MORE PRAISE FOR
TAKE BACK YOUR NEIGHBORHOOD

"A fine antidote to . . . edicts from courts that make it seem that judges think fighting crime is someone else's problem. . . . Part legal scholarship, part how-to that makes the case for vigilante groups as the best hope for reducing record levels of violent crime. . . . Urges bands of citizen patrols organized and trained along the lines of volunteer fire departments."

The Wall Street Journal

"Stunning . . . Basing his observations on experience as a legislator and Vietnam combat veteran as well as on the bench, Neely makes his case without weaseling. He earns the right to be agreed or disagreed with bluntly. His ideas deserve to be argued about everywhere."

The Palm Beach Post

"An excellent book with far-reaching ideas."

Booklist

"Fascinating . . . Intriguing . . . A pragmatic approach to law enforcement . . . Neely convincingly contends, [that] the criminal-justice system [is] inefficient and unresponsive to the society's need to deter violent crime."

The Kirkus Reviews

Other books by Richard Neely

TAKE BACK YOUR NEIGHBORHOOD

Organizing a Citizens' Patrol Force to Fight Crime in Your Community

RICHARD NEELY

FAWCETT COLUMBINE • NEW YORK

A Fawcett Columbine Book
Published by Ballantine Books

Copyright © 1990 by Richard Neely

Library of Congress Catalog Card Number: 90-86135

ISBN: 0-449-90628-0

Cover design by Dale Fiorillo

Manufactured in the United States of America

First Ballantine Books Edition: July 1991
10 9 8 7 6 5 4 3 2 1

For my father, John C. Neely, formerly Chief, Investigations Branch, Social Security Administration, who read to me reported criminal cases when I was ten years old. During the 1960s he was the only chief of a federal enforcement agency to testify before Congress against expanding wiretap authority, and he never allowed his officers to carry firearms. A kind and gentle man, I am very proud of him.

"The particular empirical event doesn't matter . . . It's an ideal principle, which can be verified only under ideal conditions. Which means never. But it's still true."

UMBERTO ECO
Foucault's Pendulum

CONTENTS

ACKNOWLEDGMENTS

Many people contributed to this book, especially the members of my personal staff. My administrative assistant, Betty Barnsgrove Price, kept the whole project together, typed most of the manuscript and did extensive proofreading. My secretary, Lea Ann Litton, gave to the project her typing, her eyeballing and her encyclopedic knowledge of the career of Don Knotts, fellow West Virginian. My law clerks, Kathleen Gross and Christopher Smith, provided much of the legal substance of the book, leaving me free to wax political. Kathleen did extensive research on the history of citizen's arrest, the recent activities of crime prevention groups and the procedures for forming tax-exempt charitable corporations. She drafted with precision the incorporation forms in the appendices. Christopher was busy on the phone chatting up Guardian Angels and other crime-fighters from coast to coast. He drafted both the text of Chapter 6 and the model statute on civil immunities, and he otherwise gave good counsel on style and substance. Christopher edited the entire book sedulously, dissuading me at every turn from butchering the Queen's English. Without him, every prison would be a "facility," every person would be an "individual" and commas would fall like rain on the just and the unjust sentence alike.

My editor, David Gibbons, made valuable contributions to both the style and structure of the book. Among other things, David constantly admonished me to be proscriptive rather than descriptive, and he cudgeled me into writing more like an advocate and less like an academic. Finally, this book would not have been published without the arduous efforts of my longtime friend and agent, Marian Young, of the Young Agency in New York. This book was difficult to place because of the subject matter. Without Marian's strong support, the book's outline and first two chapters would have ended up in my already overflowing file of unpublished manuscripts.

INTRODUCTION

The purpose of this book is to establish and legitimize community crime control. A number of communities around America have already figured out that they must take law enforcement into their own hands because the regular police are incapable of protecting them. My intention in this book is to popularize this approach to self-help so that every community may begin a neighborhood patrol and take other measures to reduce or eliminate its crime and drug threat. This is *modern-day* vigilantism. It is *not* old-fashioned, hang-'em-high cowboy justice, *not* newfangled, tear-'em-to-pieces-in-the-streets revolutionary Islamic justice and *not* standard American Ku Klux Klan put-my-white-sheet-on-again terrorism. Rather this book is about community policing organized with the same seriousness, professionalism and attention to detail that we now find among our local volunteer fire departments.

Some of the existing crime-fighting groups, like the Seattle Block Watch, are no more than traditional, passive, citizen eyes and ears for the regular police. Others, most prominently New York's Guardian Angels, are active patrollers of streets and subways who interdict crime and discourage offensive and threatening behavior. Neighborhood groups organized by Black Muslim and Christian ministers have emerged in Washington, D.C., St. Louis and Dallas to patrol streets and make life difficult for drug dealers and their clients. Indeed, the most militant volunteer groups today are either black, Hispanic or interracial coalitions. The Guardian Angels are predominantly black and Hispanic, and the militant patrollers in Washington, St. Louis and Dallas are predominantly black. Most citizen groups, however, are racially mixed, and none has anything in common with the old Ku Klux Klan, modern racist thugs or yesteryear's lynch mob.

Crime increases in direct proportion to geographical concentrations of poverty, but crime varies little, if any, with fluctuations in the economic cycle. Therefore, it is not poverty *per se* that makes criminals, but rather a complicated mix of social habits and attitudes that emerge from growing up and living in conditions of poverty and deprivation. In part, the crime rate is rising because the primary engine of social control—namely, the family—is declining. Families not only control and educate their children within a household, but with one or two working adults, families—unlike single parents—can afford to live in neighborhoods among other families. These families, even though their incomes may technically place them below the "poverty line," constitute communities that support schools, churches and other institutions that help mold the young in a positive way.

Thus, there is a difference between the "working poor," people who are struggling to support traditional family values, educate their children, strengthen their communities and improve their circumstances, and what I call in this book the "underclass." Underclass life is characterized by wide-spread illegitimacy, able-bodied unemployment, drug abuse, prostitution, welfare dependency and crime as a socially accepted means of acquiring ready cash.

Among black Americans, the illegitimacy rate is now so high (61 percent) that unless there is a major change in attitudes, ten years will see more than half of all black children living in an exclusively underclass world dominated by a criminal culture.[1] And, although the prospects for blacks are, perhaps, the most bleak among our various identifiable social groups, the prospects are also bleak for white children as divorce and illegitimacy rates rise. In 1960, 2 percent of all white babies were born to unwed mothers; in 1970, the figure was 6 percent; in 1980, the figure was 11 percent. Given the proportion of whites to blacks in the total population, the white underclass is a more prominent overall hazard than the black underclass.

In Boston, social workers report that the incidence of child sexual abuse in underclass families, white and black, is "nearly 100 percent." Between 1985 and 1986, there was a 28 percent increase in the number of reported child-abuse deaths, and although some of this apparent increase may be attributable to better reporting than in earlier years, it is unlikely that all of it is. Conditions such as pervasive child abuse in the underclass create criminals and sociopaths who then threaten the rest of society.

Those Americans who find their lives reasonably free from crime do not owe their safety to the superb police forces of the areas in which they live. Rather, they owe their safety to the fact that they have isolated themselves among other middle- and

---

[1] During the twelve months ending in mid–1987, black married women with incomes over $15,000 had fewer than 165,000 babies. During the same period, black unwed women with household incomes under $10,000 (including welfare and other government transfer payments) had 177,000 babies. *See*, M. Kondracke, "The Two Black Americas," *The New Republic*, 6 Feb. 1989.

upper-middle-class neighbors, who, in turn, have virtually no inclination to rob, burgle, mug and murder one another. But few law-abiding Americans can afford to live in communities so removed from the criminal underclass that crime is an improbable occurrence. Walled private communities with paid guards, fortress-like city apartment buildings and ritzy suburbs hours away from the nearest public housing are all prohibitively expensive. Families earning average incomes have little choice but to live in economically and socially mixed neighborhoods, which means that violent crime and property crime are constant threats.

Regular police forces rely on a reactive rather than an active model of law enforcement. The average uniformed state or local police officer spends only about 2 percent of his or her time actively patrolling. The rest of an officer's time is spent responding to calls, doing paperwork, supervising accident scenes and testifying in court. But in communities wealthy enough to hire private guards, the guards operate actively rather than reactively. Private guards devote over 90 percent of their time to patrolling and crime interdiction: People who are paying for their own protection want to prevent crime in the first place, not apprehend criminals after the fact. However, for social, political and economic reasons that I shall explore in Chapter 3, it is not possible for the public police to use the same active crime-prevention techniques that private guards use.

We know from experience that active patrolling and exclusion from a neighborhood of certain types of people—drug dealers, prostitutes, panhandlers, roving bands of adolescents and guys driving pickup trucks after midnight for no good reason—will lower the crime rate. Active patrolling will work, however, only if it is done in such force that would-be criminals appreciate the likelihood of apprehension. Exclusion of persons in the high-risk profiles raises issues of equity that are made more problematic if the neighborhood groups doing the excluding are white and the excluded underclass are black, or vice versa. This, however, is a public relations problem and not a racial problem.

Indeed, in many metropolitan areas neighborhoods are racially or ethnically segregated. A predominantly Chinese or Southeast Asian neighborhood is likely to be in the business of enforcing its community standards against its own miscreants as well as Italians from an adjoining area. The Italians, in turn, are likely to enforce their standards against blacks, and the blacks are likely to enforce their standards against whites, Asians and Hispanics. The big division today in society is not between race and race, class and class or ethnic group and ethnic group; the big division is between criminals and the rest of us. Therefore, because the necessity of enforcing standards in a community against strangers will inevitably provide opportunities for cheap-shot accusations of racism, the problem should be addressed directly. In the same way that local charities coordinate their fund-raising through the board of the United Fund, community crime-control groups should coordinate with one another and provide a way to reduce or eliminate inevitable racial, ethnic and neighborhood tensions through programs of mutual support.

The reason that neighborhoods must defend themselves is that America's high divorce rate, high illegitimacy rate, high teenage pregnancy rate and rising rate of child abuse are not problems that government can solve. Because government has been so successful since the Roosevelt administration in providing us with such benefits as social security, unemployment compensation, health care for the aged and indigent, education and interstate highways, we now believe that government is capable of solving almost any problem. The fact of the matter is that the power of government to change the way people think about themselves and to change the personal choices that people make in their own lives is quite limited.

Studies of children overwhelmingly support the proposition that delinquency, poor academic performance and emotional disability all occur more frequently and severely among children from broken homes. One recent government-supported study concludes, "The evidence that the family plays a critical role in juvenile delinquency is one of the strongest and most frequently replicated findings among studies of deviance. However, with few exceptions this evidence has been downplayed by sociologists. The motivation for the de-emphasis of the relationship between the family and delinquency is not entirely clear. [But] ... this de-emphasis appears to be in part because sociologists have in recent years tended not to see the family as a particularly viable and effective institution and to see divorce as a normal course of action for the modern family."[2]

If, indeed, not even sociologists are willing to recognize and oppose the life patterns that lead to criminal behavior, how is government to attack the root causes of crime effectively? For those who believe that law enforcement should be downplayed in favor of social services designed to uplift the underclass, I hope to prove in this book that good community law enforcement *is* a primary vehicle for social uplift. This is because communities that set appropriate standards of public behavior and exclude those who don't conform establish the basic preconditions for upward mobility in future generations.

This is not an evangelical book. Rather, this is a book for those who have already realized that government cannot and will not protect them from crime and, therefore, have already decided to take the law into their own hands. The Anglo-American tradition of citizen law enforcement is a long and honored one, and in all fifty states the lingering power of citizen's arrest is a towering monument to this ancient custom. What I shall explain in this book is how citizen law enforcement can be organized legally and effectively, with no unacceptable intrusions into our civil liberties. But, because community law enforcement is like

---

[2]W. Grove and R. Crutchfield, "The Family and Juvenile Delinquency," *The Sociological Quarterly* (Summer 1982), 301–319.

all other communal undertakings, from public schools to volunteer fire departments, I do not promise that community law enforcement can be achieved perfectly and without tension or controversy. Contrary to the assertions of ideologues, most of real life occurs somewhere between Walden's Pond and Skinner's box.

Well-to-do liberals can wax eloquent about the desirability of public spaces where everyone is free to roam. Why? Because either private space (fortified buildings and walled communities) or geographical distance (well-to-do suburbs) separate these liberals from the criminals. Blue-collar workers, on the other hand, who are at least as tolerant as the rest of us of racial, ethnic and class diversity, know better. Blue-collar workers are overwhelmingly supportive of poor people, but blue-collar workers are rightfully reluctant to allow troublemakers—prostitutes, pimps, drug dealers, muggers, panhandlers, drunks and rowdy teenagers—to roam about their streets for no reason other than to uphold a theoretical notion of civil liberties.

In the days before the civil rights revolution of the 1960s it was common for the public police to exclude the type of unwelcome visitors listed above, even if the public police did not actually patrol more extensively than they do today. Low-level criminal offenses such as vagrancy and "being a suspicious person" allowed the public police to move undesirable intruders out of a neighborhood under threat of arrest. U.S. Supreme Court decisions in the 1960s and 1970s, however, made it nearly impossible for the police to continue to perform this function. The old neighborhood control statutes were held unconstitutional, so now the police can do little to move a person on unless there is "probable cause" to believe the person has committed a crime.

I was already a sitting judge in the early 1970s when many of these court decisions were made and I heartily supported the U. S. Supreme Court because I believed that vagrancy and other neighborhood control statutes provided unnecessary opportunities for official abuse. On balance I still believe that, but I understand now that the legitimate community control function that these statutes performed must somehow be performed in another way. In the business of government we all live and learn: Often the solution to the problem changes the problem!

Today local members of community crime-control groups have no more authority to roust intruders than the regular police. And, in general, the reports of these groups indicate that their members are careful not to violate civil liberties. Indeed, like me, most members of neighborhood crime-control groups fully endorse the general philosophy protecting civil liberties. Community crime-control groups, however, do attempt to monitor the comings and goings of undesirable intruders and residents. Patrols closely follow pimps, prostitutes, drug dealers and panhandlers, so that their market is destroyed and any implied physical threat to passers-by is eliminated. Inevitably the undesirables leave for more hospitable climes, and the crime rate in the patrolled community decreases.

My observation that there are certain functions that government simply cannot perform—particularly enforcing the criminal law—emerges from years of service either in a state legislature or on a state's highest court. Every imaginable citizen group approaches government with problems whose solutions cost big money. Indeed, Americans pay the lowest taxes among the citizens of Western industrialized countries; yet, even if our tax rates were to approach those of Sweden, we still couldn't satisfy all the legitimate demands on government. Building affordable housing for the bottom 25 percent of the population, repairing America's infrastructure, improving education for children born in poverty, providing health care to the more than 30 million Americans who still haven't got it, raising to an acceptable level the income of divorced women with dependent children and modernizing hospitals, prisons and reformatories would consume any new taxes overnight.

When government officials are urged to inaugurate some new program, the most tactful way to say no is to ask the group seeking the new program what tax they suggest be raised or what other program they suggest be cut to provide the money. At the national level the traditional answers to these questions are to cut the national defense budget and to borrow the money, but at the state and local levels specific suggestions are rarely forthcoming, because the options are so limited. What states, cities and counties do is educate children, provide welfare and social services, build highways and provide law enforcement. At the state and local levels there is no highly visible, bottomless pit like national defense down which money appears to vanish for no good reason, and unlike the federal government, states can't just print money.

Law enforcement using uniformed police officers is extremely expensive. It costs at least $42,000 a year to put a uniformed officer on the street in a typical, small, heartland American city (and, according to estimates, nearly four times that amount in the major urban areas) when we include the officer's pension, disability insurance, equipment and supporting personnel. Unless one is unrealistic enough to believe that major new taxes will be imposed to support law enforcement, then the money for additional police must come from schools, social welfare, highways or health. No one is about to rob those programs to finance more cops, including even those demanding more cops, once the options have been explained to them. The alternative, of course, is volunteer action by the citizenry.

Crime emerges from a breakdown of the traditional family and traditional neighborhood. Until we restore family and neighborhood values across a broad front, crime will continue to increase. Most of the communities that today are resorting to militant self-help to maintain law and order are close to areas dominated by an underclass predisposed to crime. These predominantly blue-collar communities are not only threatened by violent crime and property crime, they are also threatened by the specter of their own children slipping into the underclass, criminal world. That is why drugs are so frightening. Honest, hard-working, blue-collar families can't pay to send their children to private schools; they can't pay to move to the suburbs; and they can't expect the already overwhelmed public law-enforcement apparatus to protect them. Therefore, some of them have decided to take the law into their own hands, and that is the most hopeful sign we have seen on the crime-control front in many a year.

The very act of organizing to protect a neighborhood from crime has the effect of strengthening traditional values concerning appropriate standards of public behavior. Because volunteer patrols have a place for adolescents as young as fifteen (if properly supervised), a community police force allows adolescents to make a clear choice between "them" and "us." A racially and ethnically mixed blue-collar community that goes to great lengths to exclude or, at least, control criminals and those likely to become criminals makes it obvious what traits are utterly unacceptable in a person—voluntary able-bodied unemployment, panhandling, drug dealing, drug abuse, prostitution, brawling, larceny and violence of any sort.

Unfortunately, there are few long-standing modern experiments in community crime control. New York's Guardian Angels have been around since 1979, and the Seattle Block Watch is about fifteen years old, but the more militant groups in Washington, St. Louis and Dallas arose only in 1989, in response to the sale and use of crack. My aim in this book is to analyze what has worked and what hasn't in those few experiments we have and to encourage more and better use of the principles of citizen crime control that emerge.

Part of the reason for the limited citizen response to crime is that to date no respectable commentator has provided historical, sociological, political and economic justifications for a community's taking the law into its own hands. America's unfortunate experience with the Ku Klux Klan, and experience elsewhere with the German Brown Shirts of the 1930s and the Chinese Red Guards of the 1960s, creates an understandable reluctance among educated and articulate Americans to endorse private law enforcement. But, as Chapter 1 will describe in detail, until the beginning of this century, in both England and the United States, private law enforcement was the rule rather than the exception. In both countries, however, it was firmly established that *punishment* (as opposed to apprehension and prevention) was *always* the work of the courts.

Therefore, although communities are already beginning to police themselves, it is important to encourage these efforts by making them socially and politically acceptable. Part of this effort involves showing where legitimate community crime control ends and the Ku Klux Klan begins. For example, a strong case can be made for community patrols' wearing distinctive uniforms and carrying defensive weapons such as night sticks and the chemical compound mace. An equally strong case can be made against carrying firearms of any sort. Similarly, it is one thing to follow pimps, prostitutes or drug dealers in order to destroy their markets and quite another to attack such persons physically.

The central focus of this book is the ancient power of citizen's arrest that has survived from the middle ages in some form in all fifty states. In most states the statutory modifications have been few, and in many states, like West Virginia, there have been no statutory modifications at all. Essentially the power of citizen's arrest means that individual citizens have as much power to enforce the law as the official, uniformed police. Citizens can lawfully take enforcement into their own hands, but they must be guided by the same legal standards that govern the regular police.

What distinguishes citizens from the regular police, however, are two attributes that make citizens more effective than the regular police: First, when properly organized, citizens have the manpower to patrol in sufficient force so that criminals believe there is a high likelihood of apprehension. Second, citizens can be active rather than reactive because they are not burdened with regulating traffic, responding to domestic violence calls, investigating crimes after the fact or doing the mountains of paperwork that dominate the working day of uniformed officers.

What follows, then, is an overview of how we can take back our neighborhoods. One day history may prove some of my arguments wrong, but we shall never know for sure until thousands of communities across the country experiment for at least a decade with different types of community crime control. The one thing we do know is that today's crime problem, which is a symptom of pervasive family and community breakdown, is becoming intolerable. I have worked hard to strike the proper balance between community enforcement on the one hand and civil liberties on the other.

Inherent in my calculations is an appreciation that this is not the 1960s or the 1970s. We solved the problem of *de jure* segregation in the United States only to be confronted by a burgeoning underclass of criminals who are disproportionately members of minority groups. The widening gap between an underclass disproportionately comprised of minorities and the rest of prosperous America threatens to undo much of the social progress of the last three decades. This is a problem that blacks and Hispanics have recognized better than whites and Asians because blacks and Hispanics are now discriminated against not so much because of race or ethnicity *per se*, but because the groups from which they emerge have developed a "criminal" reputation.[3] If unresolved, this problem is a greater threat to civil rights and civil liberties than anything I suggest in this book.

---

[3]This phenomenon is called by sociologists "statistical discrimination" and it is one of the most difficult barriers to upward mobility that minorities currently face. Unlike the discrimination of yesteryear, "statistical discrimination" is not predicated on malice; in fact, black jewelry store owners who exclude black teenagers from their

When deprived minorities begin to take back their neighborhoods, they earn the respect of the broader community and undermine the rationale for statistical discrimination. Active participation in the Guardian Angels, for example, must enhance a young member's prospects when he or she applies for an entry-level job. Those of us in politics, law and the media who make government budgets, formulate legal rules and mold public opinion, have a moral obligation to support the average hard-working American who cannot afford flight to the suburbs and has now decided to experiment with volunteer police forces.

Chapter 1 provides an historical framework and shows how private action to control crime was the norm in both England and the United States until the end of the nineteenth century. Chapter 2 explains how drugs cause other crime and why foreign governments' needs for hard currency and local employment, combined with our own graft and corruption, make it impossible to stop the drug/crime cycle without vigilantes. Chapter 3 describes why, from a political point of view, the official public law enforcement apparatus *cannot* protect us because, among other reasons, there are groups with vested interests in undermining some part of official law enforcement. Often these groups are not against fighting street crime, but find some part of the enforcement apparatus, like courts or prosecutors, a threat to their normal, legal businesses.

Chapter 4 discusses the techniques used to privatize space— walled private communities, fortress-like apartment buildings and well-patrolled suburbs—and then addresses the phenomenon

shops engage in the same type of statistical discrimination against their own racial group that whites engage in. "Statistical discrimination" emerges from the same mathematical probabilities on which we all benignly predicate so much of our personal lives. For example, we all fly in commercial airliners because the likelihood of a fatal crash is roughly one in a million. Similarly, even if we're black ourselves, we do not open our jewelry store's remote-controlled doors to groups of seventeen- to twenty-seven-year-old black males, because men in that profile have the highest statistical likelihood of holding us up.

of displacement, which simply means that the neighborhoods able to protect themselves "displace" the criminal class to other, more vulnerable neighborhoods where the people cannot protect themselves. Most academic commentators consider the privatization of space an immoral process because of the displacement effect, but in Chapter 4 I demonstrate that more, not less, privatization of space is called for. This conclusion emerges from an understanding of the limitations of the legislative process that funds public law enforcement. I describe this legislative process and its limitations in detail.

Finally, in Chapter 5, I explain what has worked in community crime control and what hasn't. In this chapter I give some concrete guidelines for organizing a volunteer police force and I address such issues as the use of offensive and defensive weapons, the value of uniforms, proper screening for "cop nut" personalities and related practical matters. Chapter 6 is a set of guidelines and forms to be used in applying for tax-exempt status, a corporate charter, setting up an organization's bylaws and developing standard operating procedures. I have also included in Chapter 6 two model statutes that will make community crime-control groups more insurable by providing them with the same immunities that the regular police enjoy, and I have included a table summarizing the nature of the citizen's arrest power (as modified, perhaps, by statute) in each of the fifty states.

Charleston, West Virginia
May 1, 1990

Chapter I

VIGILANTES IN HISTORY

When a traveler drives from Rome to Sienna on the autostrada, he passes numerous tiny towns perched on the top of manicured knolls. These are Italy's famous "hill towns," constructed during the middle ages to protect civilians from free-lance marauders. Tens of thousands of landless cutthroats were brought together by the fourteenth-century wars between England and France, and during the years of truce, unemployed mercenaries roamed Europe forming private armies that plundered and extorted any community in their paths. The hill towns are monuments to the terror the mercenary armies inspired and to the peasants' determination to protect themselves as best they could.

Going to dinner once in the old French town of Domme, I was struck by the extent to which medieval life throughout Europe had been organized around the fear of crime. Domme was built high on a bluff as a defense against raiders, and I usually can't resist speeding up the winding road from the Dordogne River to the old citadel gate. The trip takes me about two minutes, but to walk the distance without baggage would take a fit person half an hour. In the days when the road was dirt, it would have taken a peasant leading an oxcart over an hour in good weather. Yet the inhabitants of Domme daily commuted to and from their fields in the valley below—certainly a more onerous journey than our own from a low-crime area like Greenwich, Connecticut, to the financial fields of Wall Street, for instance.

Domme was founded in the ninth century as a defense against the Vikings who came up the Dordogne River from Bordeaux. Its commanding panorama gave the residents ample warning of approaching miscreants, and the difficulty of mounting the hill probably encouraged the Norsemen to look for easier pickings in the valley below. Today we make a distinction between warfare and crime, but a few centuries ago the one merged imperceptibly into the other. The distinction between common criminals and the armed forces of an invading state was entirely academic; rape, murder and plunder resulted inevitably from a visit by either.

In the middle ages there was no such thing as a local police force. Occasionally there were hired night watchmen whose job it was to stay awake while others slept, but to the extent that there was crime within a community, the entire community undertook to suppress it by apprehending criminals whenever they were discovered. Intracommunity crime was, in any event, a minor problem. The real threat came from outside marauders, and to counter that ever-present danger there were expandable armies. In fact, nearly all of medieval civilization—including such institutions as land tenure, social status, and even morals—centered in society's need to repel external threats. The most prominent aspect of society's total organization around physical security was that at the apex of the middle ages' social pyramid was a military caste composed of professional knights. Typically these knights, who are so often reviled today for the liberties they took with the peasants, attached themselves to local lords who, regardless of what they skimmed off the top for themselves and their families, were indeed responsible for protecting their communities. And if they failed, they were the first to go!

The business of knighthood required an expensive education and even more expensive equipment. It took years to learn how to wield swords, battle-axes, lances and other assorted weapons competently from horseback; furthermore, given the level of technology and the pervasive poverty, armor, weapons and horses were so expensive that together they cost several years' worth of an average family's income. Knights were expected to possess their own armor, weapons and a specially bred and trained war horse whose utility was limited to combat. A knight's charger looked something like today's workhorse; he was big, heavy, well trained and far too valuable to use except in battle. Other, lighter horses were used for transportation.

It was the knights who formed the central cadre of a medieval army, and around them ordinary burghers and peasants rallied when called according to local custom. In fourteenth-century England, almost everyone who held land—either directly from the king or through intermediate lords—held such land on condition of providing some type of military service. When the feudal hosts were summoned to battle, the great landowners brought knights, archers, foot soldiers, and provided ancillary logistical support, like horses and fodder. Lesser landlords and peasants simply rallied to their overlords by coming themselves and bringing their own provisions.

Depending upon the extent of the threat, a medieval army would be expanded by recruiting progressively less well-trained and able citizens; in time of siege, of course, everyone down to the elderly women, the sick, the halt and the lame were enlisted to repel the invaders. Usually we think of medieval society as a system of universal military service. But because medieval warfare was usually not much more than well-organized marauding on at least one side, it is perfectly proper also to view medieval society as a system of universal vigilantism.

What the Italian hill towns, the citadel at Domme and the English system of military land tenure have in common is that they reflect the extent to which "vigilantism" was the norm rather than the exception during most of human history. The reason, however, that we do not usually think of the typical medieval peasant as a vigilante is that the total organization of medieval society around self-protection was directed entirely to criminal lawlessness; it did not have a social component. Unlike the German Brown Shirts of the 1930s or our own fabled Ku Klux Klan, medieval vigilantism was not aimed at malcontents or social deviants within communities. The folks in Domme exhausted their ingenuity designing bigger and better systems for delivering boiling oil to unsuspecting Vikings not because the Vikings were pagans or wore helmets with horns, but because without the boiling oil, Domme's residents would be raped, murdered, plundered and enslaved by Viking raiders.

This abbreviated history is important because the most resilient argument against modern vigilantism is based upon a misreading of social and legal history. It is widely thought that modern society made a conscious decision that the civil rights and civil liberties of citizens would be best protected if only professional police had law enforcement powers. But the continued vitality of the power of citizen's arrest—a substantial private prerogative whose history is firmly rooted in the middle ages and is still available in some form in every American jurisdiction—proves that citizens did not abandon their rights to self-protection from anxiety about amateurs abusing law enforcement powers. Indeed, it was cupidity, pusillanimity and sloth—not idealism—that led us to entrust our safety to professional police officers. As the short narrative to follow will amply demonstrate, we delegated law enforcement duties because the average citizen is too busy, too lazy, too indifferent and often too frightened to do the necessary policing himself.

In the early centuries of English law, enforcement obligations were oppressive and something most busy farmers, artisans and merchants gratefully passed on to any alternative social mechanism available; the transfer of power was exclusively an exercise in hiring cheap substitutes instead of taking valuable time to do the job oneself. Confusion about the extent to which society made a conscious decision to repose the exclusive use of force in the state for political rather than economic reasons is understandable, however. College and law school legal history courses regularly teach that the triumph of early English common law in the twelfth century was the elimination of private warfare by according the king, through his courts, a monopoly on the use of force. Indeed, one of the great social scourges of the pre-Norman period was the private blood feud between kinship groups. Thus if John killed William, William's kin would not rest until they had killed John, and then John's kin would feel honor-bound to avenge John. Unless one enjoyed low-level warfare for the same reasons one might enjoy deer hunting, this system led to a downwardly competitive process that seriously interfered with farming, commerce and just plain staying alive.

The triumph of the king's court in the early Norman period, then, was the regularization of penalties for breaches of the king's peace—in our example, John's dispatch of William to his just reward. Under the common law, John would be hauled before the king's court, where he would be required to pay William's kin money as compensation for his crime. And there, supposedly, the matter ended, much to the satisfaction of both John's and William's kin, who could then go drinking together, marry one another's eligible daughters and generally do a lot of pleasant or useful things instead of wasting time and energy preparing for the other side's nighttime raids.

The one part of the standard received wisdom regarding vigilantism that *is* historically accurate is that a conscious decision was made to entrust the punishment of criminals to the state. Although in the twelfth century summary community punishment was still the vogue for felons caught red-handed, over the next three centuries the lynch mob became progressively more loathsome to the common law. Protection from criminal violence, however, has three aspects: prevention (when possible), apprehension and punishment. Of the three, punishment has the lowest social utility, while protection has the highest. And with regard to both protection and apprehension, early English law relied on the community at large. The entire able-bodied male populace was responsible for mounting watches and pursuing criminals when detected.

In the early Norman period (c. 1200) there were both royal courts and local (manorial) courts for determining guilt and allotting punishment, but there was no professional police force. Furthermore, although formal hanging, flogging and branding were thought the work of the judicial authorities, the notion that citizens could not use as much private force as necessary to prevent crime would have been greeted with complete incredulity. No English yeoman would have been paralysed by a sense of propriety while his children were assaulted. Thus, dope dealers wouldn't have lasted long in a medieval country town. Prevention was the province of the citizen.

Although in the thirteenth-century English law was so fiercely against self-help that it could hardly find a place for self-defense (the man who had slain another in self-defense was regularly forgiven, but he also needed a king's pardon), the law's general abhorrence of self-help did not extend to the capture of criminals. When a felony was committed it was the obligation of the citizen to raise the hue and cry (*hutesium et clamor*). If, for example, a man came upon a dead body and omitted to raise the hue and cry, he committed a criminal offense (besides leaving himself open to ugly suspicions). The proper cry was probably "Out! Out!," and when it was raised, the community was expected to turn out with the bows, arrows and knives that they were required by law to possess. Besides much shouting, there would also be horn-blowing; the "hue" would be horned from "vill to vill."

When a felon was overtaken by the hue and cry while he still had either the fruits or tools of his crime about him, he was given short shrift. If he made any resistance, he was cut down. But even if he submitted to capture, his fate was already sealed. He would be bound, and if he was a suspected thief, the stolen goods would be tied to his back. He would then be brought before some court—usually one that had been hurriedly summoned for the purpose—and without being allowed to say one word in self-defense, he would be promptly hanged, beheaded or precipitated from a cliff, often with the owner of the stolen goods serving as amateur executioner.[1]

Indeed, in the thirteenth century there was a certain resistance on the part of royal judges to the summary execution of criminals apprehended pursuant to the hue and cry, although historians assure us that the system was ridding England of far more malefactors than the king's courts. But to the extent that summary apprehension and punishment met with disapproval from the duly constituted, royal authorities, it was the summary punishment and not the system of apprehension that was frowned upon.

Toward the end of the thirteenth century, with the regeneration of urban life (which had nearly disappeared for nine centuries after the departure of the Romans) the intracommunity crime problem began to become acute. Thus, in the reign of Edward I, the 1285 Statute of Winchester provides:

---

[1]For an elaborate description of the general limits on self-help in the early law and the procedures of the hue and cry, *see* F. Pollock and F. W. Maitland, *The History of English Law*, Cambridge University Press (Cambridge, 2d edition, 1898), pp. 574–597.

Forasmuch as from Day to Day,
Robberies, Murthers, Burnings, and
Theft, be more often used than they
have been heretofore, and Felons
cannot be attainted by the Oath of
Jurors, which had rather suffer
Strangers to be robbed and so pass
without Pain, than to indite the
Offenders . . .

This statute then went on to repeat older laws and to emphasize the local community's responsibility for law enforcement. It required that the gates of walled towns be closed from sunset to sunrise, and that the inhabitants provide a night watch to arrest strangers and bring them before the sheriff. This latter provision simply reaffirmed earlier law and custom, because a royal writ of 1253 had ordered "That watches be held in the several townships as hath been wont, and by honest and able men."

The Statute of Winchester stressed the ancient responsibility of citizens to raise the hue and cry and to pursue and apprehend criminals. It also reiterated the legal obligation of every able-bodied man between the ages of fifteen and sixty to possess arms according to his station in life. To ensure the fulfillment of this latter onerous obligation (again, it should be remembered that arms were *extremely* expensive) regular inspections were instituted.[2] The persons to whom these inspections were entrusted were called "constables," and they are the same individuals who, according to the 1253 writ, were "two free and lawful men chosen from the most powerful in each hundred" who were expected to supervise the enforcement of the law.

In 1361, because of abuses of power on the part of local sheriffs to whom much law enforcement had come to be delegated, a

---

[2]I am indebted here, and for much of the history that is to follow, to the excellent work of Philip John Snead, *The Police of Britain*, Macmillan Publishing Company (New York, 1985).

new office was created, namely that of Justice of the Peace. This act of Edward III provided:

> In every county in England there shall
> be assigned for the keeping of the peace,
> one lord, and with him three or four of
> the most worthy men in the county,
> together with some learned in the law,
> and they shall have power to restrain
> offenders, rioters, and other barretors,
> and to pursue, arrest, take and chastise
> them, according to their trespass or
> offense; and to cause them to be arrested
> and duly punished according to the law
> and custom of the realm.

Soon the primary engines of English law enforcement became the local justice of the peace and his constable; both of them were unpaid, yet the low level of criminal activity in rural England permitted the system to flourish for the succeeding 600 years. Ironically, when I came to the bar in 1967, West Virginia still had a system of local, elected justices of the peace and their elected constables. By that time, both were paid modestly from court costs, and their authority had atrophied to the point where they primarily processed traffic tickets and heard civil cases involving less than five hundred dollars. As a young lawyer I found J.P.'s and constables a pretty sorry lot; most of the serious policing had been transferred to the city police forces and the county sheriffs. But on the books, until 1974, the local constable had the strongest police powers of any law enforcement officer in the state.

In rural England the low level of crime made it fairly easy to recruit prominent landowners to serve as justices of the peace. The same was not true, however, for constables: Middle-class farmers and skilled laborers could not forsake their regular occupations to undertake the onerous and unremunerative duties of constable. Yet parish males nominated to serve as constables could not refuse to serve in the position for the mandatory one-year tour of duty if appointed. The solution was that those appointed could hire substitutes to perform the actual duties, and so eventually most law enforcement came to be entrusted to deputy constables. If the portrayals of these officers by writers from Shakespeare to Fielding are to be believed, they were an even sorrier lot than I observed when I made my first foray into "Squire's court" in the West Virginia of the late 1960s.

In the cities, the Statute of Winchester, which required urban residents to mount night watches, continued in force well beyond the middle of the eighteenth century. The duties of the watch soon came to be far too troublesome, however, for the householders expected to perform them, so deputies were employed to serve as regular watchmen. Originally, the substitutes were paid by those upon whom the duty of the watch fell, but later they were paid by the parish. As with deputy constables, the pay was miserly, and the service commensurately miserable.

In urban areas, the system of unpaid justices of the peace and badly paid deputy constables and deputy watchmen had two unfortunate effects. First, the thriving criminal business drove upright citizens out of the justice of the peace vocation because, traditionally, justices held court in their houses. In the cities, the daily arrival of life's scrapings and leavings was just too much for the respectable middle class. This led to the recruitment of surpassingly venal justices of the peace in urban areas, who in turn aided and abetted the corruption of the constables.

The second effect of the English system of limited and amateur law enforcement was to precipitate an efflorescence of crime in eighteenth-century London. In fact, crime in London between 1710 and 1760 was more formidable than at any other time in Anglo-American history. As in modern American cities, the majority of the criminal class were drawn from young males who had run wild in the slums since early infancy. The residential architecture of the period, with its barred windows, stout doors and heavy shutters, is testament to the pervasive fear of housebreakers. Furthermore, in those days persons with money protected themselves; when the wealthy went out at night, they were preceded by torchbearers and accompanied by armed servants.

Across the channel, the continental cities were less crime-ridden, but that was because continental countries had standing armies that could be used for internal policing. In the England of King George II (c. 1740), any type of standing army stationed on English soil was anathema; crime was a severe problem in London, but a standing army was thought to create great jeopardy for civil liberties throughout the kingdom.[3] So, instead of a continental-style military police force, the English attempted to discourage crime by horrendous punishments, publicly administered. By the end of the eighteenth century there were over two hundred capital crimes, and the London populace was regularly presented with public spectacles at Tyburn Prison of hangings, decapitations, burnings and disembowelments.

In addition to severe and exemplary punishments, the authorities resorted to paying rewards to free-lance "thieftakers" whose information led to the arrest and conviction of felons. This en-

[3]The year 1780 saw the most severe London riots of the eighteenth century. They were called the "Gordon Riots," after a young Scottish nobleman, Lord George Gordon, who had been enlisted to lead the protesters. The cause of the riots was Parliament's relaxation of the repressive legislation against Roman Catholics, which incensed extreme protestants. Gordon led fifty thousand marchers wearing blue cockades who were originally to present a long but peaceful petition to parliament. However, along the way the protesters were joined by the perennial elements of the wild and predatory London mob, and members of both the House of Commons and House of Lords were savagely manhandled. Two justices of the peace and six constables could not disperse the violent mob of several thousand, and peace was restored only when units of cavalry were called to the scene. Nonetheless, Charles James Fox, a leader of the parliamentary opposition declared that he "would rather be governed by a mob than a standing army," notwithstanding that hundreds of people had been killed, much property had been destroyed and there had been protracted disruption of life in the capital.

trepreneurial gang of cutthroats were often derisively called "thiefmakers" because of their tendency to entrap the innocent. Nonetheless, the free-lance "thieftakers," financed as they were by reward money, became the nucleus of the first professional London police force. In 1740 Justice Thomas De Veil established his court in Bow Street, Covent Garden, then London's inner-city pleasure district, which contained theaters, taverns, gambling dens and brothels. De Veil made a fearless and resourceful attack on crime, making Bow Street preeminent among all of London's magistrate courts.

The real revolution in law enforcement, however, came to Bow Street with the arrival of Henry Fielding (1707–1754) dramatist, lawyer, journalist and author of *Tom Jones* and *Amelia* as magistrate at Bow Street. Fielding went beyond merely offering rewards to informers; he founded London's first professional detective force, which came to be known in the next century as "the Bow Street Runners." This institution flourished from the last years of Fielding's life until it was dissolved in 1839. The Bow Street Runners have always captured the imagination of historians because they were our first professional detective force, but what is truly remarkable about them was their small number and limited use as adjuncts to one modest magistrate court. Elsewhere in London, to say nothing of the rest of England, the system of law enforcement had changed little since the middle ages, notwithstanding that urbanization was proceeding at a rapid pace, unemployment was on the rise and the engines of social control that adequately governed rural, agrarian England were breaking down in the overloaded slums.

All of the problems that were prominent in the eighteenth century were exacerbated in the nineteenth century. The class consciousness and social unrest that the French Revolution created in England caused a fearful, aristocratic government to rely upon the militia and the volunteer regiments (drawn from the propertied classes) known as the yeomanry. These were the successors to the medieval peasants who were expected to practice on Sunday afternoons with their longbows. The yeomanry was primarily used, though, as we use the National Guard today—to quell severe unrest in the form of riots, not for normal police duties. When Robert Peel became home secretary in 1822 he appointed a parliamentary committee under his own chairmanship to consider police reform. What Sir Robert had in mind was the type of professional police that he had inaugurated when he was Chief Secretary in Ireland from 1812 to 1818 under the Peace Preservation Act of 1814. His Irish police, the Peace Preservation Force, had been drawn from ex-military men and had apparently enjoyed some success.

Parliament, however, was having no clone on English soil of a colonial force designed to preserve order in hostile territory. In the committee's 1823 report, the committed said:

It is difficult to reconcile an
effective system of police with that
perfect freedom of action and
exemption from interference, which
are the great privileges and
blessings in this country; and your
Committed think that the forfeiture
or curtailment of such advantages
would be too great a sacrifice for
improvements in police, or
facilities in detection of crime.

What all of this says about law enforcement is simply that a professional police force with a near-monopoly of enforcement powers has *not* always been thought to be a necessary adjunct to civil rights and civil liberties. In fact, throughout most of Anglo-American legal history, quite the opposite was the prevailing concept. The English declare to this day that a police officer is someone who is paid to do what it is a citizen's duty to do without pay.

There is no better example of this last proposition than the law of arrest. In a seventeenth-century treatise, *The Country Justice*, by Michael Dalton, there appears this sentence: "The Sherife, Bailifes, Constables and other of the King's Officers may arrest and imprison offenders in all cases where a private person may." Right down to the end of the nineteenth century in American urban areas, and down to the 1970s in American rural areas, the ideal in law enforcement was still citizen participation. However, in American cities of the nineteenth century it was hard to make this ideal a reality for reasons I shall discuss in a moment, but citizen participation was still the rule in rural America. Even today we find vestiges in rural America of the ancient justices of the peace and the local unpaid, or underpaid, constable.[4]

[4]The venality among unpaid or lowly paid justices of the peace and constables that Henry Fielding described in *Amelia* (1751) was still pervasive in their modern, West Virginia incarnations when I came to the bar in 1967. By that time, justices of the peace were paid by a system that I suppose was merely a variant of what existed in Fielding's day; justices were paid from court costs levied against losing litigants. A civil litigant could bring suit in any of a number of justice of the peace courts in a county, and the police could similarly select the J.P. court before which to bring a criminal defendant for a preliminary hearing. In my home county of Marion there were ten justices of the peace from which to choose. It didn't take a justice who wanted to make money long to figure out that if he held against the litigants who initiated proceedings in his court, he would drive all his business away. Thus, it became common lore that the initials "J.P." not only stood for "justice of the peace," but also stood for "judgment for the plaintiff."

Under the same system, the modern incarnation of the ancient constable received fees for serving civil process; but he also received fees for serving warrants on arrested misdemeanants. This, of course, provided great incentive to set up the notorious "speed traps" for which all of the South was known in recent yesteryear. In 1974 the West Virginia Supreme Court of Appeals, of which I was a member, struck this system down on due process constitutional grounds. The reason was that by giving a judge a financial stake in the outcome of criminal and civil proceedings, the litigants were denied their right to a fair trial.

In nineteenth-century America, urban police forces became inevitable. Far more than today, there were sharp antagonisms between natives and ethnics, Protestants and Catholics, whites and blacks, conservatives and radicals, and employers and workers. In the absence of rigid class distinctions, fixed neighborhood boundaries and an inclusive sense of community, many groups regarded one another as serious threats to their well-being, and the streets were, if anything, even less safe than they are today. Nonetheless, Americans shared with their English cousins a deep suspicion of professional police forces. For Americans, a national police force, like the Italian *carabinieri*, was inconceivable; a state police, like the German *polizei*, was undesirable; and, a military force, like the Irish constabulary, was utterly unacceptable. It was not until the late 1890s that there was even general agreement around the country that police officers should wear uniforms when on duty instead of civilian clothes; when New York began this process of wearing uniforms in the 1850s there was strenuous objection from the rank and file. Indeed, in mid-nineteenth-century American police forces, officers did not even carry guns or clubs.[5]

In the nineteenth century many functions concerning health and welfare that are today entrusted to specialized bureaucracies were entrusted to the police. The police cleaned streets and inspected boilers in New York, distributed supplies to the poor in Baltimore, accommodated the homeless in Philadelphia, investigated vegetable markets in St. Louis, operated emergency ambulances in Boston and were still responsible, in addition, for curtailing crime. Nonetheless, nowhere were the police thought of by the ordinary citizen as a benign force; they had enormous power that could be used arbitrarily and capriciously because all

---

[5] I am indebted here for the fine study of Robert M. Fogelson, *Big City Police*, Harvard University Press (Cambridge, Mass., 1977).

urban police forces were integral parts of the urban political machines.

The urban political machine and the urban police force nurtured and protected one another. The major source of the machine's power was its ability to provide thousands of jobs at good wages to its supporters. When the millions of poor, uneducated and unskilled Irishmen, Germans, Scandinavians, Italians and Eastern Europeans came to nineteenth-century American cities, not only could they not rise to middle-class status, but they often could find no work at all. For a full generation, and sometimes longer, they remained unemployed or underpaid, taking menial jobs whenever and wherever available. The way up to the middle class and out of poverty was to find a job in the fire, police, water and sanitation departments, courts, schools or other burgeoning municipal government bureaucracies.[6]

Urban police departments provided thousands of jobs; but they did something else that was even more indispensable to the health of the machine. They provided political money through graft. In the ethnic ghettos, gambling, prostitution, strong-arm extortion, confidence games, thievery and diverse racketeering were pervasive. Upper-middle- and upper-class natives feared the prevailing life-style and lack of morality among the impoverished immigrants. Thus they launched reform campaigns to purge their own communities (which needed little purging) and the ethnic communities of vice. They succeeded in prohibiting gambling, curtailed Sunday business, regulated saloons, outlawed prosti-

[6]This still occurs today. Astute observers of American social history from 1962 to 1989 argue persuasively that the most important effect of Lyndon Johnson's war on poverty was that it provided tens of thousands of middle-class jobs to blacks in the government sector. Although there is little debate that the war on poverty's community action *grants* did little to reduce the general problems of the ghettos through the programs they financed, they helped stabilize race relations and begin a long process of completely integrating blacks into mainstream American society by creating a solid black middle class. It is the children of blacks given a leg up in make-work government jobs during the 1960s and '70s who are the applicants to law schools, medical schools, engineering schools and graduate schools in the 1990s.

tution and otherwise imposed their own moral standards on other groups. In lower- and lower-middle-class communities these laws were regarded as unreasonable, inequitable and unenforceable.

The urban police had control over whether these laws would be enforced. This allowed them and their political patrons to share the underworld's profits and garner its political support. Furthermore, it permitted the political machine, by and through its police force, to adjudicate the ethnic and class battles over moral and cultural issues. Urban machines that controlled the police had the opportunity to implement a vice policy consistent with the prevailing life-style and underlying morality of their constituents. This situation obviously changed the role of the police from that of citizens' surrogates hired to perform the duty of citizen's arrest (because the average private citizen was too busy, too lazy or too afraid to do so) to a policy-making institution entrusted with discretionary political powers.

Probably for the first time in Anglo-American history, a distinction between criminal and social policing became important. Although the dividing line between the two is not always clear, it is essentially the same as the line between victimless crime and crime with victims. At the extremes, the difference is easy to perceive: prostitution and after-hours drinking are more or less laughing matters, whereas armed robbery causes serious concern. Yet the argument can be made that in prostitution the victim is the prostitute, and in after-hours drinking the victims are those killed by drunk drivers or awakened by late-night rowdies. Nonetheless, blurred though it is, the distinction is of central importance to the rest of this book, and it is perhaps the central consideration in analyzing the proper role of citizen patrols.

The reason this last distinction between social policing and criminal policing is important is that the consensus about law enforcement is very narrow. Everyone in a community is against rape, murder and armed robbery, while only a minority are against private poker games, illegal parking or the sale of pornographic literature. As I shall discuss at length in Chapter 3, there is a difference among social classes, ethnic groups, races and neighborhoods in the way they view the legitimacy of the regulatory laws. A citizen crime-control group that attempts to enforce laws that a majority of the community do not feel strongly about enforcing is destined to fail. The sale of drugs has now probably joined the crimes like rape and murder that almost everyone finds abhorrent, but it is hard to conceive of a citizen crime-control group that would be successful in enforcing *The Internal Revenue Code*.

The average American's ambivalence about the police is best summarized by the old saying that a conservative is a liberal who has just been mugged, and a liberal is a conservative who has just been indicted. What makes this old joke funny is its appeal to our lack of consensus about what criminal law is supposed to do. Conservatives are indicted for such activities as smoking pot, insider trading, giving or receiving bribes and soliciting prostitutes. Certainly conservatives are not indicted for muggings, armed robbery or rape! Thus, it is the vigorous enforcement of the social laws and not the laws against the old common law crimes (murder, rape, arson, armed robbery, larceny and assault) that most concerns us. Enforcement of social or moral principles taken to the extreme can engender Ku Klux Klan–type vigilantism, which in turn leads us to react negatively to suggestions of vigilantism in any sense of the word.

In this regard, the best-known example of unlawful and reprehensible vigilantism is the Ku Klux Klan, which emerged after the American Civil War as white society's special organization for dealing with blacks. There have been three Ku Klux Klans: the first Ku Klux Klan of Reconstruction times, the second Ku Klux Klan of the 1920s and the third, current, Ku Klux Klan of the past thirty years. The first Ku Klux Klan was employed to intimidate the Radical Republicans of the Reconstruction Era and, by violence and threats, to force freed slaves to accept white control. The second Ku Klux Klan differed significantly from both its predecessor and successor. Although the second Klan was founded in the South, its greatest growth occurred in other parts of the country.

During the 1920s this second Klan became a national organization and enjoyed a large following in the Southwest, West, North and East. The strongest state Klans were in Indiana, and such "un-Southern" states as Oregon and Colorado. Unlike either the first or third Klans, blacks were the second Klan's secondary target: Catholics and Jews ranked high as objects of its rhetoric, but its whippings, torture and murder were as often directed against ne'er-do-well, immoral, white Anglo-Saxon Protestants. This second Klan attacked Americans of similar background and extraction who refused to conform to the Bible Belt morality that was the deepest passion of the movement.

The Klan of recent years had neither the following nor power of the earlier two; in the 1960s its violence was directed primarily against desegregation and the civil rights movement.[7] Today the third Klan's momentum is largely spent, and its continued existence is a joint effort of not-too-bright right wing radicals and F.B.I. informants who are paid to join the group to keep an eye on the members.

Perhaps more than any other organization, the Klan is associated with American vigilantism, yet as this brief historical sketch amply demonstrates, the Klan was only peripherally concerned with anything vaguely approaching the prevention of common-law crimes. Its primary purpose was the enforcement of largely self-serving social, economic and religious norms through extralegal means. Thus, at the most basic level, the Klan has absolutely nothing in common with the private exercise of the powers of citizen's arrest by organized groups of volunteers

[7]See, Richard Maxwell Brown, *Strain of Violence*, Oxford University Press (New York, 1975).

because, while the powers of the police have always been con- gruent with the powers of the citizen, under our inherited English system, the powers of the citizen rise no higher than those of the police. And at the heart of all well-regulated police powers is the notion that punishment, as opposed to apprehension or prevention, is exclusively a judicial function. Therefore, the real problem with vigilantes is usually inartfully expressed: It is not that they will "take the law into their own hands"; rather, it is that they will act *outside* the law.

Unfortunately, this clear-cut distinction between social and criminal vigilantism has not had the practical implications in the last hundred years of American history that we might hope for. Although it is easy for legal scholars and sociologists to believe they have found law enforcement's equivalent of the Rosetta Stone once they review the history of citizen's arrest and discover the distinction between social and criminal policing, in the real world criminal policing can easily lead to social policing. This, in fact, is exactly what happened in one of the other well-known and equally reviled instances of American vigilantism: the San Francisco Committee of Vigilance of 1856.

In 1856 San Francisco was a seething cauldron of social, ethnic, religious and political tensions. The California gold rush of 1849 had brought together many nationalities—old-stock Americans, English, Scots, Irish, French, Germans, Italians, Scandinavians, Mexicans, South Americans, Jews, blacks and Chinese—who had nothing in common but a desire to profit from the gold rush boom. Ethnically, there was perhaps no more cosmopolitan city in the Western world than San Francisco in the 1850s, and on the surface, in official pronouncements, there was much tolerance and good will. Below the surface, however, there were all the ethnic tensions and hostilities typical of fast-growing cities. San Francisco was dominated by the Democratic political machine of David C. Broderick, a transplanted New

Yorker who had brought with him New York's system of ward politics. The Broderick Machine used the techniques of ballot-box stuffing, voter intimidation and precinct manipulation then typical of Eastern machine politics.

Broderick's machine had successfully overseen seven years of spectacular growth; in 1856 San Francisco had 50,000 residents and a municipal budget of $2,500,000 per year. Streets were built, wharves were constructed and municipal services were inaugurated; however, all this progress occurred at the expense of significant graft, soaring municipal debt and fast-approaching municipal bankruptcy. James King of William (that was his real name), the editor of the San Francisco *Daily Evening Bulletin*, helped crystalize the vigilante movement by fulminating against the Broderick Machine. Then an Italian-Catholic gambler shot the U.S. marshal, but was not convicted of the crime because of a hung jury. King frequently predicted his own eventual martyrdom, and six months after the marshal was shot, King's prediction was fulfilled when an Irish-Catholic political henchman of Broderick and former Sing Sing prison inmate shot him.

The shooting of King was the last straw for the reform-minded, decent citizens of San Francisco. The day after the shooting the Committee of Vigilance was formed by William T. Coleman and other leading merchants of the city. Within a matter of days the vigilantes had tried and hanged both King's murderer and the murderer of the U.S. marshal. Two months later they hanged two more men and expelled an additional twenty-eight. Thousands of San Franciscans flocked to join the committee, and soon its membership reached its highest tally of between 6,000 and 8,000 men. The vigilance committee was composed of young men in their twenties and thirties. Virtually every ethnic group, American state and European country was represented. Few Irishmen, however, were members. Leadership of the committee was held firmly by the leading merchants of San Francisco, who ran it through an executive committee of which William T. Coleman was the president with nearly dictatorial powers.[8] The rank and file of the vigilantes came largely from the city's merchants, tradesmen, craftsmen or their young employees. There were few laborers, and gamblers were forbidden to join.

The impetus to form the committee had less to do with traditional notions of protection from common-law crime than it had to do with the peculiar economic circumstances of the San Francisco mercantile class of 1856. The merchants of San Francisco depended on Eastern financial institutions for credit and, therefore, had an understandable concern for the general esteem in which their city was held. Vigilante violence was an effective way of doing in a political machine that relied upon violence and extralegal methods to perpetuate itself.

After the banishment of the Broderick Machine, the commercial classes needed some working government to put in its place. Thus the vigilance committee converted itself from an extralegal military organization to a political party almost overnight. The extralegal phase of the committee lasted barely three months—from its founding on May 15, 1856, until its disbanding with a grand review on August 18. However, its legal incarnation in the Peoples' Party lasted another ten years. Ironically, the newspaper history of the period indicates that in San Francisco during the 1850s the common-law crime problem was not out of control; almost the entire thrust of the committee's efforts was toward municipal fiscal reform. In the election that followed the disbanding of the vigilantes, the People's Party won an overwhelming victory at the polls, carrying even old Broderick strongholds by a margin of more than two to one.

[8]Here I am again relying on the excellent work of Richard Maxwell Brown, *Strain of Violence*, op. cit. *supra* note 7. Because the vigilance committee was controlled by merchants, everything was as well organized as a business. Applications to join the organization were made on printed forms, which Professor Brown reviewed in the manuscript collection of the Huntington Library.

Historians have generally condemned the vigilance committee, and the narrow fiscal focus of its successor People's Party, because it employed violence for social and political ends rather than to prevent crime. As Richard Maxwell Brown says:

Seen superficially, the San Francisco vigilantes were faced with the problem of a corrupt Irish-Catholic Democratic political machine. Their solution was to crush it. But in Broderick's approach to government, and in his appeal to the voters and his concept of municipal life, there was something more basic than boodle. At issue in the San Francisco of the 1850's were the same unresolved questions that came to typify American cities. Could extensive urban improvements be made only at the cost of wholesale corruption? In ethnically mixed cities, would newcomers of minority group status—Irish, Italians, Catholics, Jews, and others— be fully absorbed into American life, or would they be permanently condemned to economic degradation and social inferiority?

To complex problems such as these the vigilance committee's starkly simple response of hanging and banishment was tragically inappropriate—tragic for the victims, of course, but tragic also for the vigilantes who thought they were solving something when they really were not.

The San Francisco Committee of Vigilance is the consummate example of why our legal, governmental, academic and journalistic elites today share a severely reserved enthusiasm for citizen efforts to attack crime. Inevitably, vigilante movements not only create high-visibility natural leaders, but they also create well-organized followings that can potentially be used for purposes other than fighting common-law crime. Our memories of the German Brown Shirts, the Chinese Red Guards and other groups using similar means are too fresh for us not to be concerned about the attractions that paramilitary organizations have for the young, the romantic, the opportunistic and the stupid. When it comes down to it, most of us readily admit that a community of drug dealers is preferable to a community of Brown Shirts.

Typically, among the opinion-making elite, the issue of vigilante activity is framed *exactly* as the question: "Would you rather have the drug dealers or the Brown Shirts?" For most people that question is a show-stopper; at that point rational conversation about what citizens can do for themselves to prevent crime usually comes to an end. It is generally assumed that to be effective, vigilantes must operate roughly like the San Francisco Committee of Vigilance. In other words, vigilantes must go beyond the law and act in ways that the regular process of the law cannot do. But that is not necessarily the case, as a brief look at the existing powers of citizen's arrest will quickly prove.

Any citizen may arrest another if the citizen making the arrest observes a felony being committed in his presence or has reasonable grounds to believe that a felony has been committed by the person to be arrested and there are "exigent circumstances" that justify an arrest without a warrant. (See Chapter 6, Appendix A, *infra* for a state-by-state summary of citizen's arrest powers.) Typically, "exigent circumstances" are circumstances that indicate that if the person is not arrested immediately he will flee and cannot be recaptured. Furthermore, any citizen may arrest another person for a misdemeanor being committed in the citizen's presence. These are exactly the same rules that govern the police. Of course, when it comes to such actions as procuring and executing search warrants, only law enforcement officers can proceed. But with regard to the actual policing function, the power of citizens and the powers of the police are nearly or entirely the same in most American states.

There are, of course, a number of advantages that the police have over the ordinary citizen. First, the uniform and badge imply an authority that is resisted only at great peril. Female police officers are successful in arresting men twice their size because everyone knows that there is an entire force equipped with two-way radios, cars and a mighty arsenal to back up any individual officer. Second, police officers are legally armed and can resist deadly force with their own weapons. (However, contrary to popular belief, they are not allowed to gun down fleeing felons. The old line from the movies "Stop or I'll shoot!" will get an officer discharged from the force today.) Third, the police are insured against lawsuits and have a whole battery of insurance-company lawyers and government lawyers to do battle for them in court at no personal cost. A citizen who is sued for wrongful arrest might beat the rap before a jury, but he also might be bankrupted by the legal fees involved in doing so.

None of these considerations excludes the possibility of citizen crime fighters, but these considerations must be taken into account in setting up any vigilante program. And, in fact, in the biggest vigilante program in America, these factors are addressed in such a way that no one complains at all. In 1975 there were roughly 400,000 uniformed, full-time police officers at the state and local level in the United States and roughly the same number of private security guards. By 1988, however, there were 600,000 officers but approximately 1.4 million private security guards! Private security guards are simply vigilantes for the rich.

Employment as a private security guard is among the lowest status and least remunerative work available in the United States for mature, able-bodied, adult males. Although licensure requirements differ from state to state, security guards typically receive less than a total of twenty hours of training before putting on their uniforms and commencing their duties. Furthermore, except for some statutes expanding the powers of store detectives to detain suspected shoplifters until the police arrive, the powers of security guards are simply those of the private citizen. Most security guards are unarmed, but thousands of them have state gun-licenses and wear the standard police pistol belt complete with handcuffs, Mace, billy club and the regular .357 magnum service revolver. Yet with very few exceptions these security guards have never been through a police academy (typically six months of grueling work), do not drill regularly with their weapons to assure proficiency and have none of the regular close supervision that is now common in most urban police forces.

The fact that private security guards now outnumber regular officers by more than two to one is eloquent testimony to the fact that professional police officers are surrogates of the citizen. The prevalence of private security guards is also testimony to the fact that citizens don't personally fight crime because, as the English found out over a period of six centuries, it is an onerous burden that most well-adjusted people would rather pass on to someone else. The rich, of course, feel exactly the same way. The difference, however, is that the rich, living in a ritzy neighborhood in Washington, D.C., or in a high-rise apartment complex of million-dollar-plus condos on New York's Upper East Side, can afford to hire someone to perform their policing duties for them.

In my experience, hired vigilantes (security guards) have nothing in common with the Ku Klux Klan, German Brown Shirts, or the San Francisco Committee of Vigilance. In eighteen years as an appellate judge I cannot remember one case when a security guard was sued for assault, wrongful arrest, false imprisonment or even negligence. I'm sure such cases have been settled in the lower courts, but what is remarkable is the comparative equanimity with which this mercenary force of vigilantes is greeted by the community at large. The same government, academic and media elites who cluck their tongues at even such benign citizen forces as New York's Guardian Angels have nothing unkind to say about bank guards, railroad detectives or the little chap who sits in the guard shack at the entrance to Jonathan's Landing in Palm Beach County, Florida.

If the rich can protect their property, their persons and the safety of their children from criminals by hiring surrogates, the ordinary working Americans who live in declining urban neighborhoods or middle-class suburbs ought to be able to perform that function for themselves. The rest of this book, therefore, is dedicated to demonstrating why the police cannot do for us what we can do for ourselves, and how we can get serious about protecting ourselves and our loved ones, just as the residents of places like Domme and the Italian hill towns did centuries ago.

Chapter II

THE ROLE OF VIGILANTES IN THE DRUG-CRIME CYCLE

America's most famous vigilantes—New York's Guardian Angels—are about as well organized and well trained as a volunteer fire department or a group of shopping mall security guards. There are few complaints against the Guardian Angels for civil liberties violations, and studies show that the Angels' greatest contribution is that they make streets, subway stations and trains *appear* safer.[1] Patrols by vigilantes reduce anxiety and encourage a higher level of civility and public order—achievements that make urban life more endurable.

---

[1]*See* Dennis Jay Kennedy, *Crime, Fear, and the New York Subways: The Role of Citizen Action*, Praeger Press (New York, 1987). *Accord*: S. Pennell, C. Curtis, and S. Henderson, *Guardian Angels: An Assessment of Citizen Response to Crime*, Association of Governments (San Diego, CA., 1985). This latter study also assessed Guardian Angel activity in cities other than New York.

We have not had enough experience with citizen patrols like the Guardian Angels in different contexts to say definitely that patrolling will always prevent murders, rapes, robberies and housebreakings. But evidence from places like Starrett City, a middle-class housing development in Brooklyn, New York, conclusively shows that private security guards will lower the crime rate. And what security guards can do, private citizens should be able to do as well.

Starrett City houses roughly twenty thousand people in 5,881 apartments within a three-acre landfill nestled in the crime-ridden area between Canarsie, Brooklyn, and the borough of Queens. Starrett City's security force consists of fifty-five officers, who occasionally use trained dogs on foot patrols. Twenty-seven percent of households have children, 30 percent of residents are senior citizens and 62 percent are women. A comparison of the crime rates for Starrett City and the surrounding 77th police precinct reveals the following annual rates per 1,000 residents: *Murder* —Starrett City .05, police precinct .22; *Rape* —Starrett City .10, police precinct .83; *Robbery* —Starrett City 2.75, police precinct 15.51; *Aggravated Assault* —Starrett City 1.05, police precinct 6.88; *Burglary* —Starrett City .40, police precinct 15.64; and *Vehicular Theft* —Starrett City 1.10, police precinct 9.51. These statistics undoubtedly overstate the effectiveness of patrols, because Starrett City houses middle-class people who are unlikely to commit crimes themselves; nonetheless, even if we cut the comparisons by two-thirds, the negative correlation between patrolling and crime is spectacular. Furthermore, without the private patrols, the middle class would be much less inclined to live in an enclave surrounded by slums.[2]

Opportunities to reduce rude, threatening and disruptive behavior in public places and make some impact on the crime rate

---

[2]*See* L. Klein, J. Luxenburg and M. King, "Perceived Neighborhood Crime and the Impact of Private Security," *Crime and Delinquency*, July 1989.

justify experiments with citizen patrols and other forms of community policing. There is a big new problem, however, that *demands* citizen policing. The intrusion of drugs into American culture may be as cataclysmic an event for us as the arrival of bands of mercenary soldiers was for Italy in the fourteenth century. More than one in ten Americans has used an illegal drug within the last thirty days; seven in ten persons arrested for other offenses test positive for drugs. In addition, the illegal drug industry *per se* is spawning violence and savagery on a scale unparalleled in American history. Although street warfare between rival drug gangs is now limited to the inner cities, other drug-related violence is moving relentlessly to suburbs, small cities and rural towns.

Furthermore, drug trafficking is so profitable that it invites levels of official corruption that undermine our entire law enforcement apparatus. Corruption and drug-related violence are crystallizing popular support for the communities' right to police themselves through informal, self-help means. This was how America worked right after World War II; adolescent and adult vagrants who behaved in threatening ways or disturbed the public tranquility were moved along by the simple device of the roust. Although community self-help was rejected during the 1960s civil rights revolution, America today is a far more dangerous place than it was in 1960. Today it is minority residents of working-class neighborhoods in Dallas, Detroit, New York and other cities who are resorting to community self-help because the official policing apparatus has completely broken down. Unlike their middle-class neighbors, the poor can't escape to low-crime suburbs, nor do they have the power or influence to demand greater expenditures for police protection as do their fellow citizens in the stylish suburbs.

Drugs, of course, are only part of a much larger crime problem. Drug addiction, however, is our most serious crime-producing agent and is a major cause of our high property-crime rates. In some metropolitan areas as many as 80 percent of all armed robbery arrests involve addicts. One study showed that, across five gradations of increasing narcotics-use frequency (less than or equal to once per month, greater than once per month but less than daily, once daily, twice daily, and three or more times daily), approximate mean annual aggregate property crime rose from $200 to $1000, $2,700, $9,500 and $13,000, respectively.[3]

Studies of correlations between property-crime rates and the fluctuating street value of heroin have revealed a conclusive positive relationship: When the price of the drugs increases, the incidence of property crime shows a related increase. In contrast, violent crime that does not involve financial gain has shown no relationship to street heroin prices. During the East Coast heroin shortage of 1972, drops in serum hepatitis rates, an indicator of heroin use prevalence, were accompanied by regional decreases in property crime. Also, during a period of concerted effort to stem the flow of heroin into the Washington, D.C., area and attract addicts into treatment, there was a marked decrease in property crime.

All of this comports with common sense. When a person spends large amounts of money for heroin or crack, does not deal drugs himself and has no source of legitimate income, crime is necessary to support his addiction. Most addicts have had histories of arrests before their addictions. However, the coexistence of addict criminals and criminal addicts does not alter the fact that heroin and crack addiction increase property-crime levels dramatically. A high proportion of addicts' preaddiction crime consists of minor offenses, while postaddiction crime consists of serious property offenses, often involving threats to the victim's person. One study of 243 addicts estimated that they

[3]*See* G. Speckart and M.D. Anglin, "Narcotics and Crime: An analysis of Existing Evidence for a Causal Relationship," *Behavioral Sciences & the Law*, Vol 3, No. 3, 1985.

alone committed half a million crimes in eleven years!

More important, however, drug trafficking itself is making America a much more violent country. In Los Angeles, adolescents as young as fifteen roam the streets in Mercedeses and BMWs, toting Uzi submachine guns and Soviet-made AK-47 assault rifles. In 1986, there were more than five thousand violent crimes in Los Angeles—including 328 murders—directly related to adolescent gang violence. The arrival of crack in the early 1980s created a billion-dollar underground economy in Los Angeles that transformed both neighborhoods and the gangs that dominate them.

Because of drugs, gangs are no longer groups of bored teenagers engaged in petty crime; teenage gangs are now the distribution network of a state-of-the-art, billion-dollar industry. A typical Los Angeles street gang may have two hundred members between thirteen and twenty-six years old, and each gang will typically move between twenty-five and forty kilos of crack or cocaine a month. In Los Angeles County there are roughly 600 such gangs, accounting for over 70,000 active members. Although most gangs are either black or Hispanic, there are Asian, Samoan and white gangs as well. Even now, as urban markets become saturated, our small cities, suburbs and rural towns are being invaded by big-city dealers who are much more violent than the local criminals the police have been accustomed to handling.

In the small town of Martinsburg, West Virginia, about an hour and a half away from Washington by car, state and federal police arrested forty-six suspected dealers in 1986. All along the rural corridor that parallels Interstate 95 from Florida to New York, the Jamaicans have cornered the crack network. Small Town, U. S. A., offers easy profits to drug dealers at low initial risk because rural communities lack the drug awareness of big cities and are even less prepared than their urban counterparts to cope with naked savagery. Local police forces can be easily overpowered and even more easily corrupted.[4]

The unusual violence associated with all aspects of the drug business arises from a sinister combination of money, readily available hi-tech weapons and a savage portion of the underclass willing to use both without scruple. The entire drug industry reflects the sociopathic recklessness of teenagers and young adults whose poverty and deprivation have immunized them to both hope and fear; they exhibit a casual acceptance of—and sometimes enthusiasm for—torture, murder, "drive-by" shootings and public mayhem. This intense underclass savagery is partially the result of our successful integration programs. Urban ghettos no longer contain a middle class of minority doctors, lawyers, teachers, merchants and civil servants; blacks, Hispanics and members of other minorities with money and skills have moved out of the inner cities, isolating and concentrating the most desperate and least adaptable of all our people.

In Chicago, street gangs operating on drug profits have become a powerful presence, menacing the lives of nearly every resident of the inner city. They prey particularly on the single women who occupy more than 70 percent of public housing units. Gang members simply move in, take over and use apartments to store drugs and guns, turning residents into virtual captives in their own homes. Everywhere underprivileged children are telling special education teachers that classroom work is irrelevant. Why, they ask, should they struggle to learn to read and write, when they can make $100,000 a year dealing drugs? Poor children know in general terms that Americans spend from $15 to $20 billion every year on cocaine alone—money available to those courageous enough to fight, kill and be killed for it.

In Florida, the multibillion-dollar drug business dwarfs all

[4]*See* Malcolm McConnel, "Crack Invades the Countryside," *Readers Digest*, Feb., 1989.

other industries, including agriculture and tourism. By 1982, a person's likelihood of being murdered in Miami exceeded his likelihood of dying either from cancer or an automobile accident. The same statistic applies to inner-city Washington, D. C., where, in 1989, more than 400 police officers were diverted from other duties to street patrols simply to control open, drug-inspired street warfare.

Already in the Andean countries of South America, where cocaine and marijuana are produced, and in Pakistan and Afghanistan, where opium and heroin are produced, the drug dealers are better armed and better equipped than the armies and police forces expected to control them. Although North American judges, prosecutors and police have not yet been threatened, witnesses and jurors are regularly intimidated here. Few residents of Chicago's inner city are brave enough to testify about the terror to which the drug gangs subject them on a daily basis.

Ironically, self-help law enforcement is more likely to enhance civil liberties than continuing the *status quo*. Like most Americans, I do not want to be forced to urinate regularly into a bottle in order to prove I am not a drug user. Yet, I also don't want the pilot of my aircraft, the medical technician reviewing my chart or the truck driver barreling down the road at me to be high on drugs. Unchecked, drugs will threaten our civil liberties and rights to privacy because they are bringing us to a world where everyone must urinate for everyone else on command! Once we get used to that, additional intrusions into our privacy and other civil liberties will be accepted as matters of course.

Compared to the institutional invasions of our privacy and reduction in our civil liberties that the *official* war on drugs will eventually exact, an occasional intrusion into civil liberties by overzealous vigilantes is a lesser evil. The fight against drugs has already subtly changed our ancient traditions about a criminal suspect's presumption of innocence. To approve random drug testing by duly constituted authority or the erosions of pretrial rights of the accused while disapproving vigilante self-defense is to strain at the gnat while we swallow the camel.

Until recently, any person accused of a crime was *absolutely* entitled to bail pending trial because he was presumed innocent. Judges set bail for truly dangerous felons so high they couldn't make it, but before 1985 it was never admitted, except perhaps in murder cases, that some suspects are so dangerous that there can be no bail in any amount pending trial. Now, however, in the federal courts there are official guidelines, upheld by the U.S. Supreme Court, that allow a complete denial of bail to certain offenders. This has occurred primarily because of the money involved in drug running. In the early 1980s a court could set bail for drug traffickers at, say, $4 million cash; drug dealers would post the money, skip and kiss the $4 million off as a cost of doing business.

The most intractable problem in drug enforcement is the occasional user who is neither addicted to, nor even particularly in favor of, illegal drugs. College students, steelworkers, stock-brokers, high school teachers, ski bums, lawyers and even nominees to the U. S. Supreme Court may smoke marijuana or even snort cocaine if either happens to be available. But these occasional users are otherwise law-abiding citizens who oppose terrorism, graft, corruption, gang violence and the sale of drugs to children. They are, however, unwitting accomplices to murder, terrorism and corruption because they finance the drug cartels, urban gangs and arms dealers. Only a revolution from below will work. Bigger and better versions of the drug enforcement model we are currently using will simply fail on more grandiose scales.

We are losing the "war on drugs" because the lion's share of our efforts is directed to the supply side, where it is impossible to have any measurable effect, rather than to the demand side where, with vigilantes, we can probably be successful. What vigilantes can do, but the police can't, is to reduce street-level consumption significantly. The way this will happen involves two distinct processes: First, vigilantes will heighten awareness that the college students, steelworkers, stockbrokers, etc. who are occasional users are serious villains. This will occur because all of these occasional users are opposed to violent crime but are currently only dimly aware of the correlation between the crime they fear and their own tolerance for drug use. Furthermore, the person who enjoys the occasional marijuana cigarette is willing to give up his or her own pleasure only if he or she believes it will make a difference. When communities organize to fight drugs, part of that organization is mutual pledges that everyone will do everything possible to drive the dealers out, including eliminating the market by giving up individual occasional use.

Second, vigilantes will actively pursue high school pushers, break up street corner sales and even petition courts to tear down as public nuisances crack houses and other dens where drugs are used. This latter undertaking is easy when citizen crime-control groups are organized as corporations and have one lawyer, law student or even paralegal as a volunteer member. (See Chapter 6 *infra*.) Just filing the petition in court should be enough to close down the crack house.

Why, some people ask, do we not legalize drugs? Upholding the argument that drugs should remain illegal is beyond the scope of this book, but it is probably worth pointing out that widespread drug use is dangerous. A high percentage of our traffic fatalities are related to drunkenness, and for that reason organized citizens, like Mothers Against Drunk Driving, have successfully inspired a revolution from below to discourage abuse of legal alcohol. Consumption of hard liquor on a *per capita* basis has significantly declined in the United States over the past five years. The campaign against the use of illegal drugs could take a cue from organizations like MADD, which have accomplished so much in the analogous case of excessive alcohol use.

In a society dominated by dangerous machines and sophisticated technology, the possibility that other drivers, aircraft pilots, elevator maintenance men, pathology lab technicians or chemical plant supervisors will be high on drugs is too frightening to countenance. The daily pressures of living are sufficiently burdensome that drugs will always invite both unhappy children and adults to select the easy, chemical way to escape their problems. If drugs were legal we would need more, rather than less, mandatory drug testing. In essence, drugs are a public health issue and not a civil liberties issue. The present commitment of money and manpower to eliminating drugs is eloquent testimony that public opinion has firmly, if not unanimously, come down on the side of eradicating drugs.

Unfortunately, our official enforcement engines are paralyzed at the base of the drug pyramid because occasional, recreational users are a powerful, if perhaps nonvocal, political lobby. The strength of the user lobby is reflected in the passage of the Uniform Controlled Substances Act, which makes possession of illegal drugs like marijuana a misdemeanor with mandatory probation for the first offense in most states. The lack of political will to punish users has resulted in a near-universal, conspicuous policy of nonenforcement at the user level.

We no longer bother to arrest pot smokers, cocaine sniffers or even heroin addicts. If we did, we wouldn't know what to do with them anyway. In 1971, I voted for the Uniform Controlled Substances Act as a state legislator because I didn't want to see college kids sent to prison. I suspect that I would vote the same way today. Occasional users typically expect to evade detection, so we can't successfully deter most of them by putting the few we catch in prison; all we can do is randomly ruin some young lives and bankrupt ourselves building prison cells.

In rural areas, judges will send college-age dealers to prison for the first offense. In the cities, on the other hand, even repeat offenders receive probation. Fifteen years ago I believed that all drug dealers ought to be sentenced to prison. Now, however, I can see that for every ordinary street-level dealer we put away, two jump up to take his place. There are not enough prison cells to accommodate everyone caught red-handed dealing drugs, so it's probably intelligent to save what few cells we have for criminals who are both violent and deranged.

Among the strongest arguments for vigilantes is that they can reduce drug purchases without overloading the formal criminal justice system. Vigilante groups are the best engines for an extensive program of "just say no." This type of drug enforcement keeps police, prosecutors, courts and prisons from being more than peripherally involved. The way this works is that the residents of a neighborhood know who sells drugs and where they are sold. When a group of vigilantes visit the dealers, they give them the option of a peaceful departure. The next step is to swear out a warrant and help the police prosecute. Although one citizen is likely to be intimidated (and even murdered) by the dealers, it is unlikely that the dealers would take on an organized group pledged to help and protect one another.

As the Attorney General of the United States, Dick Thornburgh, said on numerous public occasions in 1989: "If we want to *lose* the war on drugs, we can just leave it to law enforcement." Indeed, Dick Thornburgh has a good handle on the problem; as attorney general, he is responsible for all our international efforts at drug enforcement. Mr. Thornburgh, a former big city federal prosecutor and former governor of Pennsylvania, is sufficiently experienced to know that most of what he does in drug enforcement is mere shadow play. That is why Mr. Thornburgh constantly reiterates the Justice Department's limited capacity to solve the drug problem. Unfortunately, Mr. Thornburgh does not go one step further and show that we are wasting our time trying to stop supply. That is the real problem: It is impossible to stop supply, which means that our current war on drugs is largely a waste of time except to the extent that confiscating some drugs helps keep prices high. In what follows, then, I hope to show that we must all reorient our efforts toward lowering demand by destroying the easy availability of drugs at the street level.

Internationally, the war on drugs cannot be won, for exactly the same reasons that the war in Vietnam could not be won. One important, but seldom-remembered aspect of the ill-starred Vietnam war was a lavishly funded effort to change the social and political system of South Vietnam. This is exactly what we are trying to do now in the Golden Triangle of Southeast Asia, Latin America, the Caribbean and other Third World drug-producing countries, but this time we are trying to do it with a lot less money and a lot fewer people. My conclusions about the futility of our efforts in curtailing Third World drug production come from my experiences in Vietnam; although all societies differ from one another, developing countries have many attributes in common.

It was over twenty years ago that I arrived in Bien Hoa as a twenty-seven-year-old army artillery captain. I was assigned to the staff of John Paul Vann, the official American skeptic about how the Vietnam war was being fought and the architect of the civilian pacification program. The South Vietnamese leadership had no reasonable expectation that their society would endure forever, or even for the next ten years. Thus, the top item on the agenda of the leadership was enriching themselves, and the primary source of big bucks was American military and humanitarian aid.

Furthermore, at every point in the system somebody had his hand out, which gave the country's rank and file little reason to support the government.[5] From the very beginnings of our efforts

[5]One example from my own experience is illustrative. By February 1969, I was in charge of economic development for III Corps and devoted most of my efforts to helping establish new industries. One scheme for which I had high hopes was the inauguration of an export-oriented furniture industry that would combine the skilled

in Vietnam, most Americans who supported the war believed that the leaders we subsidized in the South were dedicated to building a modern, noncommunist country. But although there were many South Vietnamese who shared our goals, the great majority of Southern generals, province chiefs and government officials were primarily interested in making money.

In the war on drugs we are making many of the same assumptions that we made during the Vietnam war. We assume, for example, that governments in Colombia, Peru and Bolivia share our abhorrence of the drug industry as a matter of principle. But in the Colombian city of Medellin, the local branch of the Banco de la Republica alone brings the Colombian government $600 million a year in hard currency! Notwithstanding its protestations to the contrary, the government of Colombia welcomes the drug mafia's money. And one proof of this is that the government provides a safe and legal way to launder money: Anyone can legally change cash dollars to pesos, no questions asked, at

---

labor of the Saigon area with wood brought from the excellent forests of the central highlands. Unfortunately, graft made such an industry impossible.

All major roads had government checkpoints about every ten miles. Ostensibly these checkpoints were to interdict arms and material for the Viet Cong. The checkpoints seldom turned up anything of value to the enemy, but they were treasure troves of petty payoffs. Unless a person wanted to spend all day at about 110 degrees sitting in his car or truck, it was necessary to pass the police at the checkpoint a little money for an expeditious inspection. The amount varied from a few piasters for a motor scooter to several hundred for a truck. Those with whom I was working on the furniture project determined that the volume of payoffs necessary to transport logs by truck from the area around Da Lat to, say, Bien Hoa, would be so large as to make the cost of the furniture uncompetitive.

When I raised this problem with the American bureaucracy in Saigon, I was told that I could not intrude into "military matters." Even senior civilian economists stationed in the capital discouraged my complaints about the government's self-defeating, idiotic management on the grounds that "internal regulation" was the prerogative of our sovereign client. At that point I tended to agree with the war's detractors that the Saigon government showed me little worth dying for, although I believed then, as I believe now, that the alternative was much worse. Today, of course, Vietnam has one of the lowest standards of living in the world, with an average yearly *per capita* income of $180.

the Banco de la Republica in Medellin and elsewhere in Colombia.

We currently spend $100 billion a year to fight drugs, but we have nothing to show for our efforts at the street level. The U.S. Department of Justice is proud of its leadership of the International Drug Enforcement Conference (IDEC), a consortium of North, Central and South American nations, now headed by our Drug Enforcement Administration administrator. The IDEC was formed in 1983 to conduct joint antidrug activities in the Western Hemisphere, and all the nations of Western Europe are participating observers. Some of the IDEC successes are impressive in and of themselves, but when other factors are considered it becomes obvious that arrests and drug confiscations are about as reliable a measure of success in the drug war as body counts were in the Vietnam War.

For example, in 1988 IDEC member nations carried out a coordinated effort that resulted in 1,200 arrests, the destruction of thirteen cocaine laboratories and seven clandestine airstrips, and the seizure of $3.8 million in cash as well as massive amounts of illegal drugs. In the same year we mounted Operation C-Chase, a drug enforcement sting that disrupted major money-laundering channels between the Medellin drug cartel in Colombia and the world's seventh-largest private bank, the Bank of Credit and Commerce International, based in Luxembourg. In another operation, more than 300 persons were arrested in a nationwide attack on crack cocaine gangs known as the Jamaican Posses.[6]

Yet, none of this makes any difference at the street level, which is where citizens' patrols can help. The quantity of drugs illegally imported into the United States increases significantly every year. In Medellin alone, cocaine has created twenty thou-

---

[6]The Jamaican Posses are among America's largest traffickers in crack cocaine aimed at the very young, and these gangs have staked out a significant piece of the nation's illegal firearms trafficking.

sand new millionaires out of a population of 1.5 million.[7] Cocaine wholesale prices in the United States dropped from $55,000 per kilo in 1980 to $15,000 per kilo in mid-1988. The biggest economic problem for drug dealers, ironically, is not too much enforcement, but rather too little! As University of Michigan researcher Lloyd Johnston noted in April 1988, "the supply of cocaine has never been greater in the streets, the price has never been lower, and [the] drug has never been purer." Major drug cartels with links to the governments of Third World countries are as eager as we are to keep amateurs out of the drug business in order to sustain high rates of profit.

South American drug traffickers earn an estimated $3–$5 billion each year. Latin America owes roughly $400 billion to American banks. This debt is a millstone around the neck of every Latin country, threatening both economic growth and the ability of moderate governments to survive. Thus Latin governments are caught between Scylla and Chrybdis: They desperately need new loans; they can't default on old loans without destroying their access to new credit; and, they can't pay back the old loans without austerity measures that may cause a revolution. Foreign exchange generated through drug exports is one of the few areas where they can find relief from this problem.

The cocaine industry alleviates widespread depressed conditions in the Andean region; cocaine cultivation and manufacture directly employ up to a million people. Thus, the drug industry is an important economic and political safety valve when the formal economy falters. Although Bolivia's gross national product declined 2.3 percent from 1980 to 1986, production of coca grew an estimated 35 percent per year over the same period. The official Bolivian unemployment rate more than tripled from 1980 to 1986 (from 5.7 percent to 20 percent), but so did the number of families reportedly growing coca.

[7]*See*, Tina Rosenberg, "Murder City," *The Atlantic Monthly*, November 1988.

As in South Vietnam, foreign officials will gleefully collaborate with us to the extent that they can advance their own military, economic and political goals. In some countries, like Colombia, drug traffickers have become so powerful that they can threaten the government itself—something no government willingly tolerates. What Third World drug-producing countries really want are limitations on the supply of drugs—a program similar to OPEC's occasionally successful limitations on the supply of oil—and firm control of the industry so that governments as entities and public officials as individuals can share drug profits.[8]

Governments, of course, are simply collections of individuals. Some of these individuals are brave, honest, public spirited and courageous. We regularly read about foreign policemen, prosecutors, judges and other officials who give their lives and the lives of their families in the fight against drugs. I intend in no way to disparage these brave men and women; rather, the heroes are exceptions to the general rule, which is why they are heroes in the first place. For our own policy-making purposes, however, we cannot rely on the heroes. There are too few of them, they started too late and they have too little with which to work.

[8]One systemic problem in Latin America is that governments there attempt to regulate so much that they end up successfully regulating nothing. Peru, for example, is in a shambles economically because of ill-conceived mercantile policies. Incompetent regulation has led to an enormous underground economy that is technically illegal. It is estimated that 48 percent of the employed population, representing 61.2 percent of all hours worked, engage in informal activities that have contributed 38.9 percent to the gross domestic product. Thus, the entire national economy, from top to bottom, is dependent upon technically illegal, although widely tolerated, activities. This causes severe distortions and dramatically reduces productivity. Because illegal enterprises have no official status, they cannot transfer their property easily; they cannot sell shares; they cannot convert debt into shares; they have difficulty obtaining insurance; and they are undercapitalized, because they have no access to major sources of credit. Also, these informal enterprises must disperse employees among small, inconspicuous workplaces, reducing economy of scale. In such an atmosphere, illegal drug cultivation and manufacture is but one of the many clandestine activities that keep Peru running. See, Hernando deSoto, The Other Path, Harper and Row (New York, 1988).

Indeed, there has been no change in the situation as a result of President Bush's major drug initiative in 1989. According to the State Department's annual *International Narcotics Control Strategy Report*, released March 1, 1990, "results in international narcotics control efforts were mixed during 1989." The State Department reported that the narcotics supply problem was, if anything, worse than in earlier years. "Worldwide narcotics production reached new levels, corruption undermined enforcement efforts and a number of governments still failed to exhibit a serious commitment to reducing drug production," the report said.

Twenty years ago, in Vietnam, I saw corruption similar to that associated with today's drug trade and heard all the official protestations of willingness to cooperate that we hear today. In Vietnam a military officer or civilian official was awarded and maintained his position because of corrupt alliances with officials above and below him. Money flowed upwards, and lines of authority that needed to function if the country was to be governed rationally were undermined entirely by graft networks. A province chief, for example, would have almost no control over the district chiefs in his province because the district chiefs would be corrupt partners of corps or divisional military commanders. Often we would find a province chief who was unusually enthusiastic about our pacification program. He would suggest civic action projects, like building schools or digging water wells—projects we believed would help consolidate popular support for the government. Later, however, we would learn that the province chief's real purpose in planning those projects was to divert A.I.D. cement and other building materials to the black market.[9]

Consequently, when I read about our efforts to enlist countries like Colombia in *our* fight against drugs, I have an overwhelming

[9]*See*, Neil Sheehan, *A Bright and Shining Lie: John Paul Vann and America in Vietnam*, Random House (New York, 1988) for a thorough analysis of graft and corruption during the Vietnam War.

sense of *deja vu*. In Colombia judges are not just overworked and underpaid; they are seldom paid at all. They go on strike every year to collect their salaries, and their offices frequently run out of typing paper and pens. This is a typical pattern for Third World countries: When governments are weak, they can't finance themselves. Government workers, then, are paid through graft, so that when a person wants something from the government he pays the appropriate person. Drugs generate enough money to support entire governments. It was widely reported in 1989 that the Medellin drug cartel offered to pay off Colombia's entire $16 billion external debt in return for government cooperation.

In Paraguay, military airfields, military aircraft and military personnel are routinely used for smuggling operations. Until recently these activities have involved the illegal importation of American cigarettes and foreign liquor into other South American countries, but now Paraguay wants a piece of the drug business. Paraguay makes illegal activities—including as much of the drug business as it can get—a national industry, clandestinely using *official government resources* to enhance its competitiveness.

The point, therefore, is that in Latin America and other Third World drug-producing areas, illegal activities are often carried on by the official government apparatus. Consequently, our aid to foreign governments to reduce drug production will only bring the drug business firmly under government control.[10] That may reduce supply and raise prices—both desirable outcomes—but it won't eliminate widespread drug use.

If I am pessimistic about international efforts to interdict drugs as they cross our borders, I am equally pessimistic about traditional enforcement activities here at home.

[10]Narcotics-related aid rose from 30 percent of total aid to Colombia in 1984 to over 90 percent in 1988. Congress now ties foreign aid in Latin America to recipient countries' drug eradication programs. In 1987–88 the United States withheld $17.4 million in aid from Bolivia because coca crop eradication targets were not met.

The graft and corruption that we observe in Third World countries mirror similar, if perhaps less intense, graft and corruption here at home. The 1972 Knapp Commission Report found evidence of payoffs to plainclothes police officers from gambling interests in New York City to range from $400 to $1500 per month *for each officer*. Gambling payoffs, however, are small-time when compared to narcotics-related payoffs, which run into the hundreds of thousands of dollars.

In 1982, ten Chicago police officers were convicted of taking $250,000 in protection money from narcotics dealers. A federal prosecutor was recently charged with receiving payments of $210,000 and a boat in exchange for tipping off a drug smuggler to the evidence-gathering activities (e.g., wire taps, hidden cameras) of U.S. Drug Enforcement Administration officers and to an upcoming indictment. In 1989, an F.B.I. agent was arrested in Chicago for distribution of cocaine and an F.D.A. agent was arrested for the same offense in Miami. We are not accustomed to corruption among the highly paid and highly qualified corps of federal officers.

Citizens can't monitor police and other enforcement officials. Monitoring costs are high because of bureaucratic secrecy and the size and complexity of the law enforcement process. Simply learning enough about the ins and outs of law enforcement to be able to identify a corrupt official is a daunting task even for a trained lawyer. Prosecuting attorneys and police officials have wide discretion whether to press or drop investigations, and most of the decisions they make are not put on the public record. The Knapp Commission attributed police officers' reluctance to investigate or prosecute fellow officers to "intense group loyalty."[11]

The 1987 trial of what came to be known as the Miami River Cops Case exposed police involvement in the drug trade in South

---

[11] *See*, B.L. Benson, "An Institutional Explanation for Corruption of Criminal Justice Officials," *Cato Journal*, Spring/Summer 1988.

Florida that is probably representative of corrupt activities (although, perhaps, at lower levels of violence) throughout the United States. The Miami River Cops Case began when three bloated bodies were fished out of the Miami River. According to the government's informants, the drownings were the culmination of a year of organized criminal activity by a group of uniformed Miami police officers. Trial in federal court disclosed that seven people, including one highly decorated "cop of the month," had orchestrated a series of multimillion-dollar drug ripoffs.

At trial, two Cuban drug dealers testified that they would alert the policemen to their pending drug deals. The police would then stop and search the drug buyers, seize their money or drugs and share the proceeds with their informants. In mid-July 1985, tipped off to a large drug shipment, the police sneaked into the Tamiami Boat Marina, where a boat was loaded with cocaine. As the police were hauling between three hundred and four hundred kilos of cocaine to a waiting van, they realized that the smugglers were still on board. According to government witnesses, a few officers went back to the boat, where they beat the smugglers to death and threw their bodies overboard.

This type of activity is not unique to South Florida. In February 1989, the Detroit News published a copyrighted story showing that Detroit police officers were alleged to have committed 151 crimes each year for every 1,000 officers. Allegations, of course, are cheap, but the Detroit News, availing itself of the Michigan Freedom of Information Act, found out that there were 7.2 substantiated allegations against officers in Detroit for every 1000 officers.

Other cities surveyed for police corruption were New York, with 112.7 allegations per 1,000 officers; Los Angeles, 109.5; Dallas, 65.6; Houston, 42.7; Philadelphia, 20.7; Chicago, 13.6; and Phoenix, 10.7. Houston finished first in substantiated allegations, with 12.7 per 1,000 officers; then followed Dallas, with

10; Los Angeles, 9.5; and New York, 7.5. Crimes by police a few years ago usually involved using excessive force, the *News* said. But in the past two years Detroit officers have been accused of rape, hiring an arsonist to set fire to an occupied apartment building, car theft, insurance fraud, cocaine and heroine possession, armed robbery, selling gun permits, concealing stolen property and hiring a contract killer.

It is probably fair to say that for every substantiated instance of police misconduct, there are likely to be five to ten more that were either not reported or not satisfactorily substantiated. The police are notorious for protecting one another, and notwithstanding the dedicated efforts of police internal affairs departments, investigating police corruption still presents the problem of goats guarding cabbages.

Increased instances of police corruption, of course, are directly related to the drug industry. Being a corrupt policeman has perils that must be offset for an officer to risk his career, pension, and a term in prison. Unlike profits from ordinary crime, however, drug profits are big enough to turn the head of all but the most honest officers. And there is more than enough drug money to go around: As in Miami, most of an officer's friends and associates will be sufficiently involved that no one is inclined to blow the whistle. Involvement may not include selling drugs or tipping off dealers; just protecting a friend's bar where drugs are sold is sufficient involvement to discourage an officer's moral outrage. In such an atmosphere the lone whistle-blower is likely to have a fatal accident.

People who sell drugs are usually involved in other criminal activities. Consequently, once an officer becomes involved with drug dealers—perhaps justifying his conduct on the theory that the dealers are engaged only in "victimless" crime—it is an easy step to collaborating in other criminal enterprises.

This brief exploration of why public enforcement of the drug laws, on both the international and domestic levels, is quite impossible without an unacceptable erosion of our current civil liberties, should be sufficient to convince even the greatest skeptic that vigilantes are not only appropriate, but absolutely necessary. The government simply CAN'T protect us from drugs and related crime.

Although vigilantes shouldn't act like the Ku Klux Klan or the San Francisco Committee of Vigilance, vigilantes can't be boy scouts either. Throughout most of heartland America the drug dealers aren't the Jamaican Posses or the Dominican drug gangs: the Uzis, AK-47s and M-15 semiautomatics are generally confined to Miami, Los Angeles, Chicago and a few other inner cities. Vigilantes can't handle private armies with modern weapons and shouldn't try.

But vigilantes can handle the drug dealers who hang around the school yards, sit at the back tables of local bars and stand around street corners. Vigilantes can recruit, train and support "counter gangs" for the schools. The reason that the drug dealers dominate many schools is that because of all our concerns for civil liberties, the drug dealers have a monopoly of force. But when fathers and sons, mothers and daughters, teachers and students join together and take formal oaths to support one another with whatever it takes, the days of the ubiquitous drug dealers are numbered in working and middle-class neighborhoods. In one school near Charleston, West Virginia, for example, the students themselves got together to volunteer for drug tests. They then issued IDs to everyone who passed. Although this might appear intrusive, it is also highly symbolic: It is a way of sending a strong collective message to the drug dealers who are attempting to establish markets in Charleston that they will not be tolerated. Voluntary collective action of this sort, even though it involves some coercive peer pressure, is one variant of the vigilantism I thoroughly endorse.

When school and neighborhood patrols are used, they should not attack the dealers physically (See Chapters 5 and 6 for guidelines), but they need not cower under threats against them either. Particularly in schools, where children are required by law to be, there is a common-law right to self-defense against violent law breakers. If teachers cannot or will not patrol the halls and bathrooms, there is no reason that duly constituted student safety patrols cannot, and that these patrols cannot be augmented by parents.

We need to accept either that we must protect ourselves and our children with reasonable self-help, or that we shall all be required to accept violations of our civil liberties, such as urinating on command, forevermore. And, as I shall explain in the next chapter, even with regard to rape, armed robbery and housebreaking, the official law enforcement establishment can't deliver to us what we want—namely, protection. In the United States, courts, prosecutors, police and social service agencies have simply broken down under the weight of social, economic and political forces that are only vaguely understood. As we explore these forces, the case for vigilantism will become even more compelling.

Chapter III

THE VIGILANTE RESPONSE TO THE POLITICS OF PUBLIC ENFORCEMENT

Community self-policing is much more easily said than done. Almost every American adult is busy, so even two or three hours a week of nighttime patrolling is a significant burden on his or her limited free time. Furthermore, interdicting criminals can be dangerous, particularly if unarmed citizens are more ambitious than their limited tactical training and manpower justify. Finally, there is always the possibility of a lawsuit for false arrest, assault or battery. Therefore, when I have made the suggestion publicly that community self-policing is the only answer to our rising crime problem, I have been criticized not only by social liberals who see the Ku Klux Klan lurking behind every neighborhood patrol, but by those who are simply unwilling to add patrolling to their already long list of volunteer duties.

Inevitably in discussions of self-policing the first question is why don't we improve the regular police departments so they can adequately do the job? If the United States can defend the entire free world from aggressors, why can't we also defend ourselves from our own criminals? The answer to that question leads to a discussion of complicated political, social and economic forces. The bottom line, however, is that lack of money is not the only factor that makes government law enforcement incompetent. America's law enforcement is also incompetent because all of us, at some point in the system, whether consciously, intelligently and deliberately, or not, want it to remain incompetent. That may be a counterintuitive proposition, but it is nevertheless true. In Chapter 1, we saw an example of this problem in Robert Peel's nineteenth-century England, where members of Parliament explicitly maintained that a good police system is a threat to civil liberties!

When all of us live in constant fear of violent crime, linear reasoning would imply that we immediately beef up our engines of enforcement. But protecting ourselves from crime is only one of our political goals; there are many others, such as paying low taxes, minimizing government intrusion into our personal lives and avoiding close proximity to prisons and other concentrations of the underclass in such places as work release centers or drug treatment centers. These types of considerations compete with that of personal safety for our political support. The persons who exhaust their reservoir of creative thinking about crime by pointing out that we need more police, prosecutors and prisons, would be appalled by a plan to provide those resources through a 5 percent state payroll tax! And those same persons would also be less than enthusiastic about living next to a medium-security prison or work release center. Thus higher taxes and facility location are two immediate impediments to beefing up enforcement, but problems like these are linear. We can ask people whether they want to pay for crime control or put up with the pollution of their local areas by prisons, and on those two limited subjects we can obtain a simple up or down vote.

In politics, however, it is not usually the linear obstacles to solving problems that are the most troublesome. Therefore, the average citizen is probably correct in believing that the linear obstacles to a more effective crime-control system can be overcome. A strong political will and a little creative thinking will usually solve any problem that we entirely understand. But, as we shall see in a minute, the factors that make the expansion of government crime control nearly impossible are not so obvious as funding or prison location. For example, insurance companies are unalterably opposed to creating more judgeships, because court delay helps insurance companies settle civil cases cheaply. Yet this is not a factor that most citizens concerned with better law enforcement ever think about.

In politics people are seldom forthright about what they really want or why they want it, and, in fact, outright lies are quite common to mask the motivations. Furthermore, the legislative process facilitates the obfuscation of issues and allows the hidden agendas of small but powerful constituencies to dominate policy-making. What really confounds us, then, are factors related to the unintended side effects of government policing that are largely obscure to the man in the street. Government—or the way we organize ourselves as a society—may be rational in some grand way, but it is not rational in a simple, linear way; the considerations that inform the nonlinear or seemingly illogical reasoning of government are only dimly understood.

The attractive quality of linear obstacles is that we all more or less share the same attitudes about them. There is no shame in anyone's admitting that he doesn't want to pay 5 percent more in taxes or that he doesn't want a prison built next door to his house. And because we are willing to admit publicly what bothers us about these situations, political compromises or new approaches that take account of the obstacles and give a "second best" solution to specific problems become possible. When we come to the nonlinear obstacles, however, we find interest groups that are reluctant to discuss their objections openly. This is certainly the case with insurance companies that want clogged, understaffed, incompetent courts so that civil cases take years to get to trial and with businessmen who want prosecutors' offices to be so understaffed that there are no personnel to enforce the environmental laws. Therefore, it is these nonlinear factors that make community self-policing necessary: community self-policing has few, if any, unintended adverse side effects to enrage powerful interests. Furthermore, community police organizations can bypass the standard political process that will never permit more aggressive *government* policing.

To make the difference between linear and nonlinear obstacles clear, it might be useful to leave the politics of today for a moment and look at an historical example where all the events we want to observe have already happened. The example I like best comes from the Hundred Years War between England and France. The most amazing thing about the Hundred Years War was the extent to which nonlinear considerations guaranteed that France would be raped, looted and burned for five generations by numerically inferior English forces operating at the end of a very long and precarious logistical line. Right from the beginning, the smart money said that the French should beat the daylights out of the English, but that wasn't what happened, because the smart money didn't take nonlinear reasoning in French politics into account. The French had basically the same problems defending themselves against the English that we have defending ourselves against criminals.

There were three great battles of the Hundred Years War—Crecy (1346), Poitiers (1356) and Agincourt (1415). In all three of these battles the English stomped the French through the use of tactics that the French could easily have overcome. Thus, although the first big French defeat, at Crecy, can be understood as the result of surprise, Poitiers and Agincourt defy linear comprehension. Only when we look at French society in the fourteenth century as a whole can we understand why the French refused to modernize their military so they could defeat the English war machine.

The French armies of the fourteenth and fifteenth centuries relied primarily on heavily armored knights drawn from the aristocracy. The function of these knights in battle was to terrify the opposition's untrained peasant infantry, break its ranks and then hack it to death with heavy swords and axes. At Crecy, Poitiers and Agincourt the French outnumbered the English more than three to one, but the French infantry was an untrained, conscripted peasant mob—exactly the type of troops against whom French knights would have done well. The English infantry, on the other hand, were well-trained professional soldiers, skilled in the use of the famous English longbow (which had a much longer effective range than the French crossbow and fired at least five times as many arrows per minute.) Furthermore, English infantry knew how to withstand a charge by armored knights through disciplined, in-depth formations using shields for protection and long-handled pikes for impaling horses. At Crecy, 7,000 English archers routed a much larger French force that included more than 1,000 armor-clad knights. And nearly seventy years later, at Agincourt, a mere 13,000 English soldiers armed with longbows and pikes defeated a French force of about 50,000!

Crecy should have proven that an infantry composed of trained longbowmen and disciplined pikemen would always carry the day over armored knights supported by untrained, peasant infantry. But for the French to have recognized this simple military fact would have destroyed the French aristocracy's *raison d'être* and shifted the center of military (and therefore political) power away from the landed, equestrian class toward a cadre of professional infantry officers. Such a shift would then have had the further effect of strengthening the power of the central government, because a trained professional army could be supported only by a strong, centrally directed modern state capable of raising the revenue necessary to pay the troops regular wages.

Consequently, at both the later battles of Poitiers and Agincourt, the French appeared to have learned nothing from Crecy. At both battles they again brought to the field armored knights, untrained infantry, and crossbowmen—the same combination that had so ignominiously lost at Crecy. If the goal of the French elite had been simply to field winning armies, then both Poitiers and Agincourt would have been decisive French victories. However, that was not the goal: The primary, but unstated, goal of the French elite was to maintain the social and political *status quo* within French chivalry. Thus, perhaps, viewed in this non-linear way, the actions of the French leadership were rational, but to find that rationality requires an inquiry into social, political and economic forces far removed from any battlefield.[1] The same applies to finding the rationality behind our own policies in our own wars against criminals.

In crime control we are overwhelmed by the modern equivalent

[1]Before we laugh too much at the French, it is worth noting that a similar phenomenon of nonlinear reasoning occurs in the American army. Study after study has shown that female soldiers in the American army cannot perform nonclerical, combat support missions up to the standards of men. The work is too heavy for the women's limited physical strength. However, domestic political considerations concerning job opportunities for women are a far more pressing matter in military politics than "military preparedness" for war on a conventional battlefield. Limiting women to army clerical functions would support reactionaries in the civilian economy, notwithstanding that military and civilian jobs are not in the least comparable.

The American army has many more qualified male applicants these days than available places. So it is not necessary, as it is in a country like Israel, which must be prepared for conventional warfare at a moment's notice, to use women in combat roles. Reports concerning the different performance rates of men and women in the American military are constantly suppressed by the Pentagon for political reasons; a military officer of any rank will be severely disciplined for speaking against continued use of women in the armed forces. This is because the military cannot afford to incur the political ire of the feminist movement; the army needs a coterie of active feminists to help support funding, so even if the women are militarily inefficient, in the long run they are politically efficient. *See*, Brian Mitchell, *Weak Link: The Feminization of the American Military*, Regnery Gateway Books (Washington, D.C., 1989).

of the special interests of chivalry. Just as the military results of Poitiers and Agincourt could not have been changed without disturbing social, political and economic relations among the nobility, and between the nobility and an exploited peasantry, we cannot create more efficient engines for law enforcement without disturbing relationships among our own interest groups that all of us, for different reasons, are reluctant to disturb.

Initially, it is important to emphasize that crime prevention does not involve simply hiring more policemen. Numbers of police are important, but how they spend their time is equally important. When our neighbors are having a late-night party upstairs, it is the police whom we call to ask them to turn down the music. When someone is noisily threatening imminent bodily injury to his wife and children, we call the police to quell the disturbance. The police are called out for every traffic accident—no matter how minor—primarily to provide lists of witnesses and reliable reports for later civil litigation. And, in this last regard, the police spend endless hours, paid for by the taxpayers, in civil courts testifying about what they discovered at accident scenes.

The police organize parades, lecture school children about proper highway safety and the health hazards of drugs, and the police even chauffeur high-ranking public officials around. At the end of the day, therefore, it takes little imagination to understand that for every $100 worth of police man hours we purchase with our tax dollars, only about $2 or $3 will be spent on active patrolling to prevent crime. Although theoretically that problem could be solved, from a practical, political point of view, realignment of more than 5 or 6 percent of an officer's time in the direction of active patrolling is nearly impossible. Domestic disturbances are important, and so are traffic accidents where, in civil litigation, millions of dollars are often at stake.

Finally, in our legalistic criminal law system, where civil

liberties are correlated with due process, and due process is correlated with meticulously following complicated procedures and providing appropriate documentation, it is difficult to reduce an officer's paperwork load. Given the logic of and the political pressure for a "reactive model" of police response, and the glacial pace at which entrenched bureaucracies change, it is difficult to envisage police departments radically altering their way of operating.

Therefore, accepting that the average uniformed state or local policeman now spends only 2 percent of his or her time patrolling, and that increasing that percentage beyond perhaps 5 percent is nearly impossible, it is easy to recognize the futility of spending more money on additional officers. If we spend big money to augment police forces so that policemen can do more paperwork, appear more frequently as witnesses in court, interfere more frequently in domestic quarrels or set up more speed traps, we haven't solved our protection problem, but we've spent a lot of money buying services we don't really need. And the average voter simply doesn't *want* to pay for more paperwork, traffic enforcement or domestic advice.

More portentous, however, than the fact that additional police will not necessarily result in more patrolling, is the fact that more police will require an augmentation of other government agencies that handle malefactors after the police have apprehended them. Additional police are useless without more prosecuting attorneys to prosecute offenders, more judges to hear the cases, more probation officers and social workers to prepare pre-sentence reports and supervise convicts diverted from prisons, and more prisons, mental hospitals and juvenile schools to receive the offenders we commit to public custody. All of this expansion costs a load of money, but cost is only one of many considerations that guarantee there will be no significant change in the existing public enforcement machinery. Therefore, we must now turn our attention to the real reasons why special interest groups (which, ironically, for the most part favor better law enforcement with regard to violent crime) oppose policies to augment public enforcement.

Let us start, then, with an examination of the courts—a bottleneck though which all criminals must pass if the deterrence aspect of the criminal law is to be effective. One would think that with our general loathing of violent criminals, criminal courts would be so efficient that they would operate like packing plants sending meat on its way to dressing and processing. We all know, of course, that courts don't work that way, yet there is little enthusiasm for expanding the number of judges available to hear criminal cases. The criminal courts in every major city are so overburdened that defendants are guaranteed favorable plea bargains as incentives not to clog the system by demanding time-consuming jury trials.

According to a classic study by the staff of the New York *Times* in January 1981 (their findings remain true for what happens in all major American cities today), hardly any of the persons arrested on felony charges in New York City are ever prosecuted and convicted as felons. New York Police Department figures showed that the chance of a person arrested for a felony being sentenced to prison was one in one hundred and eight. Although many cases can be explained away by "overcharging" on the part of the police, the largest number of avoidances of prison sentences come from the prosecuting authorities' willingness to permit felons to plead guilty to lesser charges. This willingness to cut deals favorable to defendants is a direct function of the limited judicial resources available to give jury trials and the chronic understaffing of the prosecutors' offices. In 1979 there were 104,413 felony arrests in New York City, of which 88,095 cases were dismissed and 16,318 indictments procured. Of those indicted, 56 percent pled guilty to felonies (but often less severe felonies than those with which they were originally charged), 16 percent pled guilty to misdemeanors, 12 percent were dismissed after indictment, only 13 percent went to jury trial and 3 percent resulted in some other disposition.

The reason for utter incompetence in the judiciary, however, has little, if anything, to do with decisions about the value of trying defendants charged with violent crimes. The real problem—entirely of a nonlinear nature—is that courts are *not* just *criminal* courts; courts that process criminals are almost always civil courts as well. For example, a New York State general jurisdiction trial judge is not just authorized to hear criminal cases; he can also hear all types of civil cases ranging from simple automobile accident cases to multiple party, multibillion-dollar product-liability cases. The same is true of any federal district court judge.

One way to decide many issues that arise in the civil courts is to make the courts so clogged, overburdened, complex, expensive and incompetent that no decision can possibly emerge in any reasonable time. That decides everything in favor of the *status quo*, and the *status quo* is exactly what many powerful interest groups really want. Lack of a concerted effort to improve the courts, far from being simply a function of legislative parsimony or governmental inattention, is actually a reflection of general contentment among those possessing political power with a system that does not work very well.

When, for example, civil courts work efficiently, the net result is that plaintiffs as a class prosper to the detriment of defendants as a class. In cases pitting working people against insurance companies, employers or manufacturers, courts are simple machines that redistribute wealth from those who have money to those who don't. If the machine breaks down, no wealth can be redistributed, and this is obviously a positive economic benefit to individuals and institutions with money.

Business interests (which have disproportionate power in the United States Senate because of the enormous expense of state-wide senate campaigns and senators' reliance on political action committee [PAC] contributions) would be totally misguided to support the creation of additional federal judges. Keeping federal judges busy all day long presiding over criminal trials is a far more effective method of reducing business's overall jeopardy to judicial wealth redistribution than changes in the substantive law. But this is not the type of political position that civil defendants talk about publicly. In fact, defendants regularly encourage their lawyers to serve on bar committees whose ostensible purpose is to improve the courts, reduce delay and fix the system. The insincerity of these efforts is obscured by the rhetoric contained in voluminous reports and pompous bar association pronouncements that have no effect whatsoever on the real world of day-to-day politics.

Civil plaintiffs such as accident victims need money today, not money ten or fifteen years from now when the courts get around to disposing of their cases. Therefore, when available judges are so overwhelmed with criminal cases that the civil docket moves at a glacial pace, civil defendants—particularly insurance companies who are regularly sued as a normal part of their business—are able to settle cases for ten cents on the dollar. It takes little imagination, then, to recognize that any proposed legislation that would augment the number of trial court judges would be opposed by civil defendants. However, opposition is never articulated in terms of the effect new judges will have on expediting civil cases; it is always articulated in terms of the "cost" of new judges and their supporting staffs.

Courts, however, are not unique among our public enforcement engines in being the target of hidden political agendas. The hidden agenda problem is even more prominent with regard to prosecuting attorneys and their staffs. If we create more prosecutors to go after armed robbers, murderers, rapists and dope dealers, the additional personnel will also be available to go after those who commit consumer fraud, antitrust violations and political corruption. Although the political establishment in most places is genuinely against murder, armed robbery, rape and dope dealing, the typical political establishment is less enthusiastic about prosecuting consumer fraud, antitrust violations or political corruption. The political establishment, in fact, may be involved in these activities themselves.

Because prosecuting attorneys are usually elected and, therefore, have political aspirations, they are inclined to play to the press by crusading against white-collar crime and political corruption. Efforts to increase staff for the prosecution of violent crime—a universally well-regarded undertaking—became impaled, then, on the justifiable fear that the same prosecutorial staff who can take aim at members of the underclass can also take aim at members of the country-club set who make political payoffs, rig elections, pollute the air or perpetrate frauds on consumers. Furthermore, it is not possible to rely on sound prosecutorial discretion to provide a solution to this problem, because all of the incentives to any politically ambitious prosecutor encourage country-club prosecutions at the expense of robbery, murder, rape or drug prosecutions.

The newspapers and TV stations get bored with run-of-the-mill, violent, underclass crime, but they go into ecstasy over the prosecution of the humblest white-collar criminal. The reason is simple: Newspapers and television stations are private, profit-making companies that are in the *entertainment* business and not the information business. The for-profit media find enormous entertainment opportunities in white-collar prosecutions which are middle-class morality plays that assuage the average reader's or viewer's personal sense of unrequited merit. It's great entertainment to watch Ivan Boesky go down in flames, but not so enthralling to see the mundane armed robber sent up for ten to life.

The upper echelons of American society—businessmen, politicians, lawyers and government officials—are acutely aware of the extent to which they are the targets of envy. Government regulation now is so pervasive that it is nearly impossible to carry on normal business or government activities without running afoul of some low-grade criminal law. Furthermore, the anti-corruption statutes—particularly the federal statutes prohibiting conspiracy, mail fraud, extortion (Hobbs Act) and organized crime (RICO), have been so liberally construed by pro-prosecution federal judges, that an ambitious federal prosecutor can indict almost *anyone* under one of these statutes and either win a conviction or literally bankrupt the defendant with legal fees. At the state level there are similarly vague statutes presenting opportunities to procure easy indictments.

Furthermore, statutory crimes like conspiracy in restraint of trade, illegal water pollution, running overweight trucks on public highways or speeding should be distinguished from good old-fashioned felonies like murder, rape and armed robbery. Everyone agrees that we want vigorous enforcement of the laws against violent felonies, but huge segments of the population favor passive resistance to the newer statutory offenses that are part of our efforts at economic and environmental regulation. Whole towns, for example, whose livelihoods depend upon the survival of obsolete industrial plants, may conspire to violate the environmental laws, and millions of motorists now equip their cars with radar detectors and CB radios so that they can violate the 55 or 65 m.p.h. speed limits on interstate highways. Society is composed of diverse groups with diametrically opposed interests; these groups attack one another more or less viciously in the political process. When one group wins a political battle, a statute is passed prohibiting something that another group wants to do. In turn, the losers continue the political battle by undermining enforcement of the offending statute. Thus, passive resistance to regulatory laws is not always limited to elites: There are big differences in attitude about highway safety between the northeastern urban middle class and Wyoming truck drivers. For the truck drivers, highway safety simply lengthens hours and reduces income.[2]

The attitude of both truck drivers and business elites about the legitimacy of the regulatory laws is neither irrational nor reprehensible. The problem for society as a whole, however, is that the exact same machinery that is used to protect us from violent felons is also used to enforce the regulatory laws that many people like truck drivers and business elites believe are unjust and should be resisted. It is for this reason that I pointed out in the first chapter that vigilantes must confine themselves to enforcing only those laws against violent crime, property crime and drug dealing about which there is nearly universal consensus. Otherwise, vigilantes become involved in politics and invite serious political retribution.

At this point it is worth taking into account the different experiences and perceptions of the crime problem by different social classes. Criminal victimization studies show that a person's likelihood of being a crime victim is strongly correlated in a negative way with income. In general, poor people are victims and rich people are not. The likelihood of a woman from a family making under ten thousand dollars a year being raped is almost four times greater than the likelihood of a woman from a family making forty thousand dollars a year or more being raped.

The same correlation occurs in property crime. Rich people

---

[2]For example, if those favoring temperance among college students succeed in passing a statute prohibiting beer distributors from delivering kegs directly to fraternity houses, then the beer distributors retaliate by having their friends in the legislature cut back the funding for the beer commissioner's enforcement staff. If there are but two beer inspectors for an entire state, distributors can deliver beer to fraternity houses for years without getting caught. When they do get caught, they can take a month's suspension, pay a small fine and simply write the episode off as a cost of doing business. Such a battle, albeit within the government's regulatory scheme, cannot logically be thought to be about "crime." All the participants, as well as all the spectators, understand full well that this particular battle is only about politics.

live either in suburban neighborhoods or in well-patrolled, well-fortified city buildings. The underclass is discouraged from visiting either place by some combination of geographical distance, social distance, private security and community vigilance. Because the lion's share of the people who determine how many prosecutors we will hire have more or less solved their own crime problems through private expenditures—buying either geographical distance or armed guards—they perceive prosecutors more as nuisances and menaces than as crusaders against our common enemies.[3]

The result, then, of this widely shared and, to an extent, justified dislike of prosecutors is that prosecutorial staffs everywhere will continue to be overworked, underpaid and undersupported logistically. As the crime rate continues to rise relentlessly, it is inevitable that prosecutors' offices will not be able to sustain even the current inefficient ratio of prosecutors to criminals. Regardless of what our governing elite say in their public utterances, they are largely content when young, ambitious prosecutors are so busy trying murderers, robbers, rapists and drug dealers that they have an acute shortage of time and resources to enforce the regulatory laws.

The attitude of America's elite toward prosecutors is the same attitude that the middle and blue-collar classes have toward the police. Police are by nature bullies as well as heroes, but the smaller the police force, the more police officers tend to exhibit the characteristics of heroes rather than of bullies. The average guy on a bar stool intuits that the more uniformed officers we hire to crack down on crime, the greater the likelihood that his civil liberties will be abused. Although the guy on the bar stool may not be able to explain it quite this way, at some gut level,

---

[3]The portrait that Tom Wolfe draws of his state prosecutor in Chapter 29 of *The Bonfire of the Vanities* is not only entirely accurate, but it is also the way most members of the business, professional and political elites perceive prosecutors.

he suspects that work in any bureaucracy will expand to fill the time allocated to do it, and that among available work opportunities, public employees will always select the easiest. If police are not busy with serious crime, they will inevitably meddle in activities like private poker games and speeding on the interstates, where no one wants their "help."

Blue-collar workers become most aware of the police when officers are enforcing the speed and parking laws. Minor moving violations these days typically cost between sixty and one hundred dollars in fines and court costs. This is no insignificant sum for a working family. When I was a state legislator I served on a number of conference committees that were banging out differences between the Senate and House versions of bills to raise the pay of state policemen and increase the number of officers. The increase in officers would have lowered the burden on existing officers, who traditionally worked twelve-hour days with few holidays, short weekends and no overtime. Among legislators in both chambers I found that the state police were universally supported by the rural members and universally despised by the urban members.

The reason for this strange difference in attitude was that in rural areas the state police spent their time driving pregnant women to hospitals, coming out in the snow to jump-start stalled tractors and trucks, and investigating serious crimes. In the cities, on the other hand, ambulances and garages did the useful things that the state police did in rural areas, so the average citizen's experience with the state police was limited to seeing them set speed traps, ticket vehicles for not having inspection stickers and roust late-night revellers at after-hours bars. When I was a legislator I had a high regard for the state police, which was why I was selected for the conference committees. But I seldom got the troopers the money they deserved, and to get them any money at all, I always had to trade away the proposed increase in manpower.

State legislatures, county commissions and city councils are made up of ordinary people whose attitudes closely mirror those of their constituents. And the average person is entirely unenthusiastic about a pervasive police presence because he doesn't want to pay a hundred bucks every time he runs a yellow light or makes an illegal U-turn. However, what the average person does want is a supremely efficient reactive police force that is there quickly and competently whenever needed. This, basically, is what the state police gave our rural residents, which was why the rural residents supported them. In the cities, however, there was too much policing for the average person's taste. Aside from patrolling to prevent larceny and violent crime, the average person is happiest when the police stay out of sight until summoned for a citizen-initiated purpose. This is why it will be impossible to change the current reactive model of policing. Active patrolling to prevent violent crime inevitably ends up with enforcement of the U-turn laws, which no legislator will ever tolerate.

In the first chapter, I pointed out that the police have always had broad discretionary power in enforcing moral standards. How much gambling, prostitution, drinking and drug selling a particular locale will tolerate is largely a matter of police and prosecutor discretion. This means that what type of police force a particular locale has is a matter of supreme importance to the purveyors of vice. And for that reason, purveyors of vice have little in common with ordinary criminals like burglars, armed robbers, car thieves, rapists and arsonists. While ordinary criminals avoid normal social intercourse and isolate themselves among other members of the underclass, the purveyors of vice are surpassingly active participants in the *political* community. In my own experience, the purveyors of vice have much more political influence than the local chamber of commerce, and the thing they most want from the political process is bad law enforcement. On many occasions I have actually seen the vice interests (which, of course, are allied with other criminals, like the ones who fence stolen goods) actually elect their own local prosecuting attorney.

My first job as a teenager was in the circulation department of the old *Maryland Gazette* in Anne Arundel County, Maryland. Anne Arundel County is a suburb of Baltimore that includes Maryland's capital city of Annapolis. In the late 1950s, when I lived in Anne Arundel County, the atmosphere was more southern and rural than it was suburban and cosmopolitan, and the county still had legal slot machines in food markets, drug stores, gas stations and restaurants—a phenomenon observable nowhere else on the East Coast at the time. My first boss at the newspaper, a brilliant, disbarred lawyer who had once been Maryland's secretary of state and later fell from grace in some kind of scandal, helped me enormously with his willingness to teach me whatever he could about business and politics.[4]

The one situation, however, that my first boss tried to explain to me that I could not understand at the age of sixteen (but understand now after twenty-one years in politics) was why Anne Arundel County couldn't or wouldn't outlaw slot machines— devices that invited impecunious housewives to squander scarce household money on whirling fruit. The answer, of course, was that the gamblers shared their ill-gotten gains with the politicians. Whenever a person filed for elective office in Anne Arundel County or even elsewhere in Maryland, he received an unsolicited campaign contribution from the slot machine owners. "What would happen," I asked, "if a person ran for the legislature on a platform of abolishing slot machines?" My boss replied in a way unfathomable to me at the time: "He'd get a campaign contribution from the slot machine operators anyway!"

Needless to say, that answer was counterintuitive, but my boss was unshaken upon cross-examination. At one point in this conversation I asked what would happen if a young reformer simply refused help from the gamblers. My boss's response was that one morning the reformer would walk onto his front porch and find a bag with five thousand dollars in unmarked fives and tens.

Twelve years later, when I began my own political career, the inherent if counterintuitive logic of this strange *modus operandi* became obvious to me.

The fact is that few people are much interested in local elected politics. When I ran for office, it was difficult to get anyone interested in meeting me; it was more difficult to get anyone to give me campaign money; and, it was even more difficult to get anyone to volunteer man hours to my campaign. Leaders of the teachers' association and the local unions acted like United States senators at a Supreme Court confirmation hearing: They were suspicious inquisitors who, under the best of circumstances, could be enlisted as only reluctant allies! The middle class would hardly deign to shake my hand in a department store or on a street corner, and other people who were active in politics—Democratic executive committeemen, local office holders and employees of state and local government—usually had relationships with incumbents that precluded helping a young challenger like me.

The one place, however, where I found political help generously forthcoming was from the purveyors of vice.[5] All the gamblers, bar owners and suppliers of illegal slot machines to the American Legion, VFW, Moose Clubs, etc. were extremely

[4]I worked happily and enthusiastically for this gentleman for three summers while in high school. Therefore, when I applied to Dartmouth College it was natural for me to ask him to fill out the college's form for a character recommendation. I have always found it a singular honor to be an Ivy League graduate whose character recommendation for entry into that old boy network was written by a convicted felon! On another level, however, as a criminal judge I have always thought that this ironic circumstance has helped my perspective.

[5]I hasten to point out here that in my part of the world in the early 1970s drug dealing was not an accepted part of standard, innocuous vice. In fact, one of the *quid pro quos* for general toleration of prostitution, gambling and illegal drinking was that none of the established local vice purveyors be involved in drug dealing. Once when out-of-state drug dealers decided to experiment with the Marion County market, they were met by some of the local underworld characters at the border and told to move on. Such drugs as were sold in those days—mostly marijuana—were sold by amateurs at the local college or free-lance dealers who were pursued relentlessly by the authorities and disowned by the traditional vice lords.

supportive. They introduced me to their friends, got their wives to hold coffees for me to meet the local ladies, contributed a little money and encouraged their associates who worked the polls to put me on their slates. In later years I figured out that this was because they expected me to win anyway. But they never asked me how I felt about the state liquor laws, whether I believed that prostitutes should be prosecuted or what I thought about illegal slot machines or numbers games. Unlike the teachers, labor unions and local business groups, they did not want any express promises signed in blood and under oath.

Ordinary citizens who simply want honest, efficient and even-handed government are numerous, but they are not very active in election campaigns. The active participants in elections are those who want specific policies from government that will benefit themselves. In an election campaign for prosecuting attorney in which the purveyors of vice have a friendly candidate, that fact does not necessarily come to public notice. Today elections are won with technological fire power like television advertising and direct mail. All that is needed to obtain this technology is money. The purveyors of vice are much more generous campaign contributors than ordinary honest citizens, and their campaign contributions are funneled through sources that appear legitimate. Furthermore, even city councilors, county commissioners and state legislators are disproportionately supported by organized forces that have an interest in keeping enforcement personnel at a minimum.

These organized forces, then, are joined by entirely honest citizens who are cynical about the police's crime-fighting abilities (there's never a cop around when you need him!) and are reluctant to be ticketed for parking or stopped for speeding any more frequently than is currently the case. State legislators and city council members can always find more interesting and politically rewarding ways to spend money than on police and supporting staff salaries. Finally, none of the resistance to more police is necessarily irrational or reprehensible. As I have already pointed out, a small percentage of the time of any new officer is likely to be spent patrolling neighborhoods, rousting unsavory characters or protecting our persons and property.

Our cynicism that more police will not necessarily lead to more patrolling is justified. No matter how many policemen are available, there will always be more calls than any reactive model can handle, which means that the average cop will still spend only about 2 percent of his time patrolling. This 2 percent is essentially the amount of time available between calls, during down time, or simply when the cops are reluctant to do more arduous work. If the police are *not* out roaming our neighborhoods, that fact does not impress itself upon our consciousness. But, if the police fail to come when we call them, we get angry enough to make trouble for elected officeholders.

Most of us have stopped calling the police for anything less serious than a rape in progress or a burglar entering our basement window. The reason is that when we do call the police, there is little they can do that is useful, or they come so late that there is nothing they can do. Often, indeed, if the police come in time, they are so unhelpful that we wish we hadn't called them in the first place! Yet as soon as there are more officers, there will be more calls: Police officers are a "public good" that is offered free of charge to all citizens on an even-handed basis. Because there is no fixed price for this good, the demand always exceeds the supply. Certainly this is what would happen if a grocery store gave away free steaks; the store would have more takers than it could possibly have steaks.

Usually, supply and demand establish a market price for a given item, and in this way the item is rationed. Absent such conditions, rationing is accomplished in other ways—either by the political process, as it was during World War II with the issuance of ration cards, or by standing in line, as it is with tickets to rock concerts or college football games. Police are rationed both ways. In general, the political authorities provide more police per resident to middle- and upper-class neighborhoods because those neighborhoods have disproportionate political power. That well-observed and frequently criticized phenomenon, however, is simply the beginning of a complex rationing system, the most important part of which is rationing through priorities set by the police themselves. Thus, the police usually respond reasonably expeditiously to information about a rape or bank robbery, but complaints about domestic violence or loud neighbors elicit only the most leisurely responses. Citizens who are willing to stand in line for a long time, then, get the largest share of discretionary police time and effort. And, for this very reason, those of us who are impatient about standing in line or have something more profitable to do than sit around waiting for an officer (who will inevitably look something like Millet's "Man with a Hoe") usually don't call the police about minor problems.

Squads of police who do nothing but patrol to prevent serious crime *could* be organized, but limiting their activities to preventing murder, rape, armed robbery, larceny and, perhaps, drug dealing would require a frank admission that we don't really want serious enforcement of the traffic, vice and regulatory laws. I might be willing to accede to that proposition in a general way, but I personally draw the line at lax enforcement of the drunk-driving laws. (Perhaps this is because I have young children.) Someone else, on the other hand, may not worry so much about drunks on the road, but he might be fanatical about the 55-mile-per-hour speed limit to conserve limited fossil fuels. A third person might be relatively indifferent both to drunks and speeders, yet have a well-justified hatred of noisy, stereo-playing teenagers in his neighborhood who cause him more grief than any criminal. More police, then, inevitably evoke an extraordinary political hassle about how they should be used. When, however, police are few in number, their rationing is based on simple priorities mixed with a first-come, first-served principle that has limited capacity to stir political controversy.

So far we have focused briefly on three aspects of the public enforcement system—namely, courts, prosecutors and police— that are perceived as anything but benign by large, overlapping segments of our politically active population. I have chosen to dwell on the seldom-articulated, self-interested reasons for gutting these enforcement engines because this self-interest inspires the most powerful resistance in the real political world. There is one further argument that should, at least, be mentioned, although its proponents appear to be declining in number as the sixties generation enter middle age and become family-oriented conservatives. Nonetheless, a sizeable number of citizens in the United States still believe that crime is directly related to the structural injustices of this society and that such resources as we have should be devoted to attacking crime's "root causes" and not simply to alleviating the symptoms.

Thus, it is thought by many that poverty, unemployment, racism, disintegration of families and lack of public education are the real culprits, which means that social policy should be directed toward providing criminals with education, housing, jobs and counseling rather than more policing and prisons. Many of those who hold this particular view are distanced from every-day crime threats (Tom Wolfe's "limousine liberals"); however, sociological studies show that even in the slums, where rates of criminal victimization are highest, there is broad support for the "root causes" thesis. Whether the thesis is correct makes little difference for our purposes; the very fact that it enjoys such broad support adds one more obstacle—this time an obstacle arising from idealism rather than self-interest—that blocks any bolstering of the public enforcement machine.

The root causes lobby does exert a positive political influence, however, in the area of providing facilities to receive offenders before or after they have been processed by the courts. With regard to courts, prosecutors and police, objections to augmentation based on cost are easily quelled because in fact reducing crime has a strong positive economic effect. But when it comes to either punitive or rehabilitative facilities, cost is the overwhelming consideration. Aside from facility location there are few negative considerations that stand in the way of better treatment or longer punishment.

To build and operate acceptable prisons, hospitals and juvenile schools will severely strain our resources, and that fact alone implies that if police, prosecutors and courts were *more* efficient, we would be unable to receive all the new malefactors whom they managed to capture and convict. The shortage of adequate prison, hospital and juvenile facilities is short sighted, but this shortage makes community patrolling even more necessary. This is because patrolling discourages crime in the first place, which then reduces the strain on already overcrowded facilities. No crime, no apprehension, no conviction, and thus no sentence! It's as simple as that.

At another level, community patrolling inevitably introduces the probability of community apprehension. If things follow their natural course, community patrols will be staffed by the same people who serve as volunteer firemen, sit on juries and coach little league football. These people are not thugs. Rather, they are the backbone of our tolerant, generous and liberal society. Much of the crime that most annoys us is not committed by professionals, nor by armed and savage members of the underclass. Rather, it is committed by young men—often, but not even usually, minority young men—who have few prospects for making honest livings. It is also committed by bored teenagers who have been left to run wild in the streets because their families either can't or won't give them the guidance and support they need. The only difference between a harmless runaway teenager and an accomplished juvenile criminal is about two weeks on the street. Survival opportunities for homeless adolescents are limited.

Rehabilitation is not entirely a liberal illusion. I have seen apparently hopeless cases turned around by competent social service agencies. Often, if young criminals are shown a little attention, support and even affection, their lives can be changed for the better. And just as the police have wide discretion about whether to arrest an offender they catch, so the local community patrol would have the same discretion. Fourteen-year-old vandals can be treated entirely differently from adult rapists and muggers.

Crime is strongly correlated with sex, age and race. In general there are few female violent criminals—so few in fact that my home state, West Virginia, for instance, does not even have its own medium or maximum security penitentiaries for women. Of male criminals, by far the majority are between sixteen and twenty-seven years old. And, finally, blacks and Hispanics commit proportionately more crimes than whites and Asians. Intervention, then, among young males has the highest likelihood of reducing the crime rate.

In West Virginia we have one excellent school for boys between fourteen and eighteen who have serious behavior problems of the aggressive, violent, acting-out variety. Among these adolescents, over half suffer from an inability to read. When a child can't read and do simple mathematics, all opportunity for advancement is foreclosed to him or her. Consequently, children with learning disabilities get quickly turned off by the schools and become more and more alienated and hostile.

Teaching children to read and reckon, finding them after-school jobs and putting them in the company of good role models who can lovingly teach them how to succeed in life are natural offshoots of community patrolling, just as they are natural offshoots of the regular public enforcement system. Because of the shortage of public resources for remedial training, counseling and just simple personal attention, the public facilities usually get children after it is too late. A good facility with a high staff-to-inmate ratio doesn't get a child on his first breaking and entering; rather, it gets him after he has violated probation three times and has been caught in an armed robbery. At that point a young person is quite far along in a life of crime and it becomes all that much more difficult to turn him around.

Community intervention with failing adolescents on the other hand, is an integral part of community patrolling and it can prevent things from going too far along in the development of potential criminals. The reasons why this is true should become obvious as we proceed to the next chapter and focus on the politics of public funding.

Although this chapter may appear slightly cynical, it is impossible to make the case for vigilantes without showing just how low the political common denominator is in our law enforcement consensus. Indeed, the bigger the political subdivision making the decisions about law enforcement, and the greater the class, ethnic and racial diversity in that political subdivision, the lower the likelihood that any particular neighborhood will be protected without hiring private guards or patrolling itself.

The real value of community crime patrols, then, is that such patrols can devote themselves entirely to the lowest common denominator about which everyone agrees. In this regard, community crime patrols (just like private security guards) are not concerned with illegal parking, unauthorized U-turns, private poker games, uninspected motor vehicles, political corruption, rigged elections, consumer fraud, environmental transgressions or violated building codes. Therefore, no political interest group perceives community crime patrols as threatening, so community crime patrols have no effective political opposition. Furthermore, the volunteers in these crime-fighting organizations have no political constituency to satisfy other than themselves. That means that their time can be spent being active rather than reactive; they are not at the beck and call of any particular interest group or segment of the community.

Finally, volunteer community crime patrols provide an enormous return on any money invested. Regular police officers are extremely expensive. In addition to their salaries, regular officers are covered by disability and family medical insurance; they receive pensions after twenty years of active service; and they are supported by a long logistical tail of secretaries, radio operators, laboratory technicians, mechanics, administrators, review boards, etc. This means that it may cost as much as a hundred and fifty thousand dollars a year in big cities to put a uniformed officer on the street. When, however, a local government decides to appropriate a mere fifty thousand dollars to a community crime-fighting organization, or to support such an organization with in-kind contributions of equipment such as radios or regular officers for training, the potential return dwarfs all alternative ways of spending the same money. Volunteers should be insured against lawsuits for battery and false imprisonment, and also for death or disability incurred while patrolling. Otherwise, all volunteer man-hours are free. And every man-hour is spent patrolling or backing up those who patrol.

Any augmentation in the official policing apparatus, including prosecutors and courts, will immediately inspire political opposition from those with hidden agendas. But no one will oppose government support of community volunteers as long as they act like volunteer firemen and not like Ku Klux Klansmen. This, then, is the crux of the argument for community enforcement: It is not that community enforcement is the *best* alternative for controlling crime; rather, it is that community enforcement is the *only* alternative for controlling crime.

Chapter IV

THE MORALITY OF PRIVATE SPACE

The most difficult obstacle to better public law enforcement is that the people who have the highest need for protection have the lowest capacity to pay taxes. Conversely, the taxpayers who can pay for public law enforcement can also isolate themselves in suburbs, fortified buildings and privately patrolled neighborhoods. Property crimes, most of which are covered by insurance, are the crimes that the tax-paying upper-middle class suffers most regularly.

Statistics conclusively prove the perfect negative correlation between crime victimization and income. In other words, the less money one has, the more likely one is to be a crime victim.[1]

[1] *See*, for example, M. Hindelang, M. Gottredson and J. Carofalo, *Victims of Personal Crime: An Empirical Foundation for a Theory of Personal Victimization*, Ballinger (Cambridge, Mass., 1978); *BJS Data Report*, 1988, U.S. Department of Justice, Office of Justice Programs, Bureau of Justice Statistics (Washington, D.C., 1989).

Crimes involving theft and jeopardy to the person are much more likely to occur as a potential victim's income falls. Gas stations, fast-food restaurants and all-night markets, for example, are the most frequent targets of armed robbery, and these are the establishments that pay low wages to unskilled workers. Furthermore, there is a higher statistical incidence of violent crime being perpetrated on racial minorities than on whites, even when income factors are held constant. This is because members of minorities are more likely to live in or near poor neighborhoods than whites of comparable incomes.

Violent crime perpetrated upon strangers and property crime, in terms of who commits these acts, is strongly correlated in a negative way with social class. Bank vice presidents who spend their evenings raping women in city parks, high school teachers who commit armed robberies during the school breaks and nurses who burglarize apartments when off duty are real rarities. Social class is partially a function of income, but it is even more a function of values and lifetime habits. Thus, a third-generation welfare client does not become middle class by winning the lottery, and a regularly employed white-collar worker does not become lower class when he is disabled and becomes permanently unemployed. That it is class and not income which best predicts the likelihood of crime can be gleaned from the fact that crime is strongly correlated with geographic concentrations of poor persons, but only weakly correlated (if at all) with the economic cycle.[2] One reason, then, that middle-class neighborhoods have such low crime rates is that so few criminals live there. In middle-class neighborhoods the greatest crime threat comes from strangers or from the neighborhood's own adoles-

The Department of Justice compiles voluminous statistics on all aspects of crime annually and now even has an "eight hundred" telephone number, (800) 732–3277, so that Justice Department staff can give immediate statistical help to researchers.

[2]See, Edwin H. Sutherland and Donald R. Cressy, *Principles of Criminology*, 7th ed. rev., J. B. Lippincott Co. (Philadelphia, 1966).

cents—the residents of the neighborhood with the lowest level of internalization of middle-class values and the shortest period during which to have developed middle-class habits.

Looked at one way, the most important function of a prison is to incapacitate criminals so they can't get at us. Therefore, why waste perfectly good and very expensive prisons on criminals when we could live in them ourselves? After all, good steel doors, fortified walls and armed guards can keep the criminals out just as effectively as these security devices can keep them in! Long ago, the residents of places like Domme or the Italian hill towns decided that they would live in the prisons and let the Vikings and the marauding mercenary bands forage for themselves in the countryside. But what about the law-abiding Frenchman or Italian who wanted to live on his farm in the countryside? The answer was that he couldn't do it and remain safe: That's why farmers had the long commute from their homes on tops of hills down the winding roads to the fields below.

In rich towns like Palm Beach, Florida, where the price of real estate (two million dollars an acre and up) effectively excludes not only the poor but also the middle class, it is possible to have a superb, publicly financed police system. In such a community everyone agrees that the purpose of the police is to keep undesirables out, and in so doing to recognize the difference between true undesirables and either the employees or customers of the residents. In Palm Beach, the public police officers are well paid and generously supported logistically by local tax levies to perform the protective and preventive functions through active patrolling that sometimes appear insensitive to civil rights and civil liberties. The crime rate, however, is negligible in Palm Beach, and local juries generally support the police in their occasional in-court clashes with the underclass. Even the Palm Beach parking regulations, which limit street parking to those residents with permits, are designed to make it nearly impossible for lower-class nonresidents to linger without paying stiff fees which, of course, rich tourists can easily afford.

A woman who winters in Palm Beach and spends the rest of her time in Washington, D. C., would be reluctant to support Washington's police force as lavishly as she does Palm Beach's. In Washington such support would simply be money down the drain, from her private point of view. Even if her municipal taxes were doubled in Washington, there would be little improvement in her own level of protection. Indeed, because of her private wealth, our Palm Beach snow bird can protect *herself* when she has to be in Washington far better than the corrupt and lackluster Washington police. Washington, in fact, is so poor and so mismanaged that, in August and September of 1989, the police ran out of rape kits for preserving evidence in sexual assault cases. When TV station WUSA broke the story, the police couldn't understand what all the fuss was about. "We run out of pencils, too," said a department spokesman. No one who could do better would want anything to do with a police department so underfunded that it can't even preserve, much less uncover, evidence of serious crimes.

A wealthy resident of Washington, then, would naturally want to recreate a replica of Palm Beach right in downtown Murder City so that she would have no need for the official police. The best way to do that would be to create a pleasant little prison through the privatization of space: If our rich woman could find two hundred other rich people, then the safe thing for her to do in Washington would be to custom-design a community, with a high wall, armed guards to exclude the unwelcome, a tightly monitored entry gate and active patrols to make sure nobody has gotten through the barriers. Of course, if this intrusive type of surveillance, patrolling and identity-checking were done by the regular police on public streets it would violate constitutional rights. But in a private community, residents can contract with one another for whatever degree of intrusion they are willing to accept on their own property, and then enforce that contract among themselves. Furthermore, these types of arrangements make the absence of such items as publicly funded rape kits a matter of indifference because the residents of such communities are never raped. Thus, private action can and often does solve public problems, but only when there is private money in quantities that working-class Americans can't afford.

The increasing prevalence of limited access, walled communities is an intelligent response to crime. Indeed, it is just one part of a general trend toward the "privatization" of space. Not all privatization of space, however, is the result of a crime threat. Much privatization, such as shopping malls, emerges from entirely benign considerations like economies of scale. Nonetheless, once space is privatized for any reason, use of private-property rights to create an exclusive environment becomes the natural next step. During the 1989 Christmas season, for example, there was a major brouhaha in Cleveland, Ohio, over the exclusion of Salvation Army bellringers from Cleveland's three largest shopping malls. This was a serious blow to the financing of a worthy charitable organization, but the exclusion of solicitors follows logically from the control inherent in shopping-mall architecture, where access by public streets is no longer necessary.

The urge to privatize space, however, has now gone beyond legitimately private space and entered the public sphere. Even in areas served by public streets we are beginning to see the barricading of neighborhoods. In sections of Miami and Fort Lauderdale, for example, private guards control checkpoints and lower gates to stop cars. Constitutional objections are met by the argument—erroneous, I believe—that the barricades are lawful because all motorists are detained and, in principle, allowed to enter, after drivers have answered questions and had their license numbers written down.

Real privatization of space with limited access, walled communities patrolled by paid guards and the quasiprivatization of space—such as we already see in Miami and Fort Lauderdale—have an unintended, sinister side effect. This side effect is called by sociologists "displacement," which simply means that the aggressive patrolling of some neighborhoods displaces crime to other, more vulnerable neighborhoods that are less able to protect themselves.

For example, in New York City, car owners have recently begun to enter into contracts with the city police to waive the constitutional rights that protect them from illegal stops, searches and seizures (those, in other words, made without probable cause) between 1:00 A.M. and 5:00 A.M.—the hours during which most automobiles are stolen. Motorists who have agreed to this waiver arrangement (something that I would certainly do if I lived in New York) place two yellow decals on their rear windows, indicating a willingness to have their car stopped, searched and the driver identified for absolutely no reason during nighttime hours. This project has greatly reduced the theft of vehicles with the yellow stickers, but the project has had absolutely no effect on the overall rate of vehicle theft. Therefore, all the project has done is displace auto theft from those who are willing to waive constitutional rights to those who either are not willing to waive constitutional rights or don't understand the project.[3]

We know that displacement is a serious problem in private crime control but we don't know the problem's exact dimensions.[4] Bored adolescents in working-class or middle-class neigh-

[3]*See*, G. Marx, "An Increase in Individual Aggressive Countermeasures?" *Crime and Delinquency*, July 1989.

[4]My training in economics leads me to believe that all correlations between private policing and displacement are like the old money-supply equation where, according to economists, money times its velocity of circulation equals prices times the number of transactions—$MV = PT$. The equation tells us that if we increase the money supply without changing the speed at which people spend money (velocity), we will get either much higher prices (inflation) without any increase in transactions, or (what we all

borhoods who would ordinarily break, enter, steal and vandalize for kicks, but who are deterred from so doing by visible and active patrolling, will probably not go elsewhere to commit crimes. In that case, then, private policing achieves a net positive result that makes everyone better off. On the other hand, the unemployed junkie who must support a $200-a-day crack or heroin habit will leave patrolled neighborhoods in search of easier targets. In this second case there will be no net positive result, but merely a displacement of the bad guy from a neighborhood that can protect itself to a neighborhood that can't. This means that the underclass will concentrate in neighborhoods that are so disorganized that they can't protect themselves, which, in turn, will heighten victimization among the poorest and most vulnerable of our population.

The tendency to privatize space, even if such privatization involves nothing more sinister than private community patrols (with all that implies in excluding the underclass), is something that is decried by all thoughtful commentators, both liberal and conservative. For example, Charles Murray, a Bradley Fellow at the conservative Manhattan Institute for Policy Research in New York and author of the famous critique of the American welfare system, *Losing Ground*, recently wrote:

> Let us draw together the various strands
> —the aging of the baby-boomers, the failure
> of the new wave of liberal programs, the
> demise of "structural unemployment," the
> racialization of AIDS, the unmooring of
> liberalism itself.
> For years, the black inner city has been
> the symbol both of America's past failures
> and of its obligation to admit blacks to full

want) a lot more transactions without significantly higher prices, or both more transactions *and* higher prices. But the Federal Reserve can never know in advance what will happen until it pumps a few billion bucks into the system and waits a year.

equality—and it has also been an object of
fear, anger, and guilt. Over the next few
years, specific and quite powerful trends
will effectively diminish the guilt and
increase the fear and anger—especially among
liberals. By the mid-1990's, what is now a
more or less hidden liberal condescension
toward blacks in general, and toward
the black underclass in particular, will have
worked its way into a new consensus.

The particular form the new liberal
consensus will take depends on circumstances,
but in general mainstream liberal
intellectuals and policy-makers will have
become comfortable believing something like
this: (1) inner-city blacks are really quite
different from you and me, and the rules that
apply to us cannot be applied to them; (2) it
is futile to seek solutions that aim at
bringing them into participation in American
life, because we have seen that it cannot be
done; and (3) the humane course is therefore
to provide generously, supplying medical
care, food, housing, and other social
services—much as we currently do for
American Indians who live on reservations.
And so we will have arrived in the brave new
world of custodial democracy, in which a
substantial portion of our population,
neither convicted as criminal nor adjudged to
be insane, will in effect be treated as wards
of the state.

. . . Such views would then become the baseline
from which other, still more extreme measures
to segregate the underclass could be
contemplated.[5]

[5]C. Murray, "The Coming of Custodial Democracy," *Commentary*, Sept. 1988.

The big argument against private protection, then, follows largely along the lines of Charles Murray's dire warnings about custodial democracy. If, indeed, a large number of the stable communities figure out a way to privatize their space and effectively exclude the underclass, the inner cities and housing projects will, in effect, become concentration camps populated by nothing but criminals and those noncriminals so down and out that they have no choice but to live among the criminals. This, indeed, is a serious concern, but there are ways of addressing it that are more effective than simply abjuring private law enforcement. In general, private law enforcement works and public law enforcement doesn't; therefore, the practical solution, if not the ideal solution, is to bring private law enforcement to the honest poor rather than taking it away, as a matter of theoretical equity, from everyone else.

The reason that private law enforcement works better than public law enforcement is that: (1) private law enforcement is designed to prevent crime rather than investigate and prosecute crime after the fact; and, (2) private law enforcement is largely contractual, just like private covenants limiting the number of houses per acre, forbidding multifamily occupancy of neighborhood houses or prohibiting the building of shacks on front lawns in classy residential districts.

Opponents of private law enforcement raise the specter of a police state where everyone's comings and goings will be monitored by electronic surveillance, pass checks and restricted access. Opponents are also fond of quoting Benjamin Franklin's observation, "They that can give up essential liberty to obtain a little temporary safety deserve neither liberty nor safety." Well, that sounds good, but everything is a matter of degree. I absolutely refuse to have a television monitor in my bedroom, but I'm happy to stop at the gate of a private community or have my car checked between 1:00 A.M. and 5:00 A.M. Americans, in general, are good at drawing lines: We still know the difference between drinking a little wine with dinner and becoming a falling-down drunk.

Therefore, I would argue, the proper model for law enforcement is widespread privatization of space, combined with active community patrolling. Notwithstanding the imperfections in the theory of such a system, we know for a fact that such a system will work, and we also know just as surely that the current public policing system does not work. It is, after all, eminently stupid to build a bigger and better model of a system that doesn't work.

At the heart of the difference between what does and does not work is money, pure and simple. Private security, combined with the privatization of space, costs less than available public alternatives because with it crime doesn't happen, which means there are no losses of property, no injuries from violent attack and no felons to convict and punish. Public enforcement, on the other hand, is bankrupt because it allows crime to occur and then can't afford to punish the few offenders that it happens to catch. In the last chapter, I cited the dismal figures on felony prosecution rates in New York City which showed that few apprehended felons are actually prosecuted and convicted as such. Court congestion, lack of prosecutors and lack of jail space to receive those convicted absolutely demand that courts and prosecutors allow most felons to plead to lesser offenses—misdemeanors or minor felonies. New York is typical of all large cities, and it is conceivable today that the prosecution and punishment rates in Boston and Washington are even *more* appalling than they are in New York.

Among academics who devote themselves to social science, the standard approach to the inequity inherent in neighborhoods' and social classes' differing abilities to protect themselves is to maintain firmly that we need to bolster *public* enforcement, improve social services (not a bad idea) and discourage both intrusive civil-liberties-destroying security measures and the privatization of space. All of that would be commendable in a world where it is possible in the practical sense, rather than imaginable in the theoretical sense, to do these things. As I explained in the last chapter, however, it is simply impossible, for both political and fiscal reasons, to bolster public-sector enforcement. The theoretical "perfect solution" offered by the academics doesn't work and never will. It is for this reason that I selected the quote from Umberto Eco to open this book. What's left for us, then, is some "second best" solution that comes close to achieving what the perfect solution would achieve, but without the political and fiscal obstacles inherent in implementing the perfect solution.

Therefore, let us experiment with some second best solutions and see how close they can come to achieving the ideal results of the perfect solution. One solution is to figure out how welfare mothers, their dependent children, the elderly poor and the mentally disturbed homeless can join the upper-middle class in private and commodious "prison" environments. For example, there is no reason why a public-housing project can't enjoy the same type of limited access, privatized space and private security that a good upper-middle-class private residential community enjoys. But arranging such a community requires enough political will to say that criminals may not live in public housing. It also requires enough political will to prohibit criminals from visiting public housing unless they're on their best behavior. (Indeed, criminals visit Palm Beach all the time.)

This is simply to say that if a public-housing resident has criminal visitors, that resident is out—no "if's," no "and's," no "but's." The response, of course, is outrage from the social scientists, because the suggestion has such limited prospects for success in the real world. But, ironically, unless I miss my guess, the suggestion has a lot more likelihood of success in the real world than the entirely ridiculous notion that somehow we can protect the honest residents of the Chicago and Los Angeles housing projects with traditional public-policing. Now you talk about ridiculous, that's *really* ridiculous.[6]

Nonetheless, one is certainly entitled to ask, where will the criminals not currently incarcerated live? The answer is that they'll live with all the other Vikings and marauding bands of hooligans somewhere deep in the city jungle or the countryside. I, for one, don't care where they live or where they visit, as long as it's not anywhere near me or anyone else—regardless of income—who chooses to avoid them. Indeed, the reason that public housing is such a hellish place to live is that we lack the political will to discriminate between the deserving poor and the criminal underclass.

[6]Publicly run housing projects are not the only vehicle we currently have for providing subsidized housing to the poor. In the 1970s, the Department of Housing and Urban Development inaugurated a program that subsidized private developers willing to build and manage housing to be rented to the poor. The program was popularly known as "section-eight housing," a name taken from the section of a larger statute that created this particular program.

In section-eight housing a private owner rents apartments to the poor, who pay some set proportion of their monthly income—typically between twenty and a hundred dollars—toward their rent. The federal government then pays the difference between what the poor person can pay and the fair market value of the apartment. Ideally, efforts are made to get middle-class tenants to live in the complexes, as well as the poor, but for numerous reasons starting with the acute shortage of housing for the poor and ending with the reluctance of the middle class to live with lower-class neighbors, these efforts have seldom been successful. Obviously, there are far more poor persons wanting these apartments than there are apartments to go around, so it is difficult to get into a section-eight project. More important, however, it is difficult to stay in.

The private developers who run section-eight projects cannot afford to allow vandalism, infestation of pests or rowdy behavior likely to lead to property damage or liability for the developer. Consequently, there are *very* tight rules and regulations for living in a section-eight project, and those who violate the rules are immediately evicted. Indeed, the courts have tended to be more sympathetic to the tenants of section-eight projects in eviction proceedings than to the tenants of exclusively private apartment complexes, but even with the greater government regulation and due process rights for tenants because the operation is government sponsored, there is much more order and a significantly higher level of maintenance in section-eight projects than in the public-sector ones. So, privatization of space not only can be done, it actually has been done.

Whenever a visitor goes to a place like Kiawah Island,[7] South Carolina, for instance, he informs the gate guard whom he plans to visit. The gate guard calls the resident, confirms that the visitor is authorized and then admits the visitor. The resident, then, is responsible for the good behavior of his visitor. I enjoy living in places like Kiawah Island, and I doubt that my attitude about the trade-off between mildly intrusive security and supreme physical safety would change if I were a resident of a Chicago housing project. On the other hand, I would not want to pee in a bottle as I entered the gate at Kiawah Island, and I also wouldn't want to do so upon entering a housing project.

Unfortunately, a person living in a housing project probably has a slightly different mix of friends from a person living on Kiawah Island, and that presents problems. It is difficult for peace-loving, law-abiding poor people not to have friends and relatives who are criminals. (The same problem is shared by professional politicians.) But the rule must be that one simply cannot have visitors who make trouble. One's children, on the other hand, are a different matter. Even on Kiawah Island (or in any other ritzy neighborhood), there are adolescents who make trouble, and that's something we all have to live with. But when the children get entirely beyond control, then they and their families must go. Simply put, an environment's high quality is a direct function of the methodical exclusion of undesirables and of mildly intrusive, but nonetheless voluntary, security screening.

The argument in favor of expanding private space and private security as a matter of public policy doesn't make any sense, however, until the utter bankruptcy of the public system for

---

[7]Kiawah Island is a year-round ocean-front resort located about twenty-five miles southeast of Charleston. It is composed of thousands of condominiums and several hundred expensive detached houses. Most people who own apartments live elsewhere and rent their apartments out when not vacationing in them themselves.

incapacitating dangerous felons is completely appreciated. Since 1968, the prison population of the United States has more than tripled. We currently incarcerate a higher percentage of our population than any other industrialized countries except the Soviet Union and South Africa. About 3.4 million people, or almost 2 percent of our nation's adult population, are in federal, state or local custody. The number of adults in the United States on parole rose 11 percent from 1986 to 1987, while the number of adults on probation rose 6 percent over the same period.

As of 1989, thirty-six states were under court orders to relieve prison overcrowding. We require new prison beds at the rate of one thousand every week! Taxpayers adamantly refuse to pay for new facilities, in spite of the truly hellish conditions in the old ones, and few communities are willing to have prisons built nearby.[8] One major reason for this is the number of underclass camp followers who are drawn to a prison where husbands, fathers and sons are incarcerated. These relatives of inmates enter the welfare rolls, increase the community's crime rate and gen-

---

[8]After years of efforts by the judiciary in West Virginia to encourage the executive branch to take prison reform seriously, the West Virginia Supreme Court of Appeals finally declared in December 1988 that the conditions at Moundsville Penitentiary—our maximum-security prison—were so substandard that the prison would be closed in 1992 regardless of whether there was another facility to take its place. However, to ensure that a new prison would be built, the court decided, in a related case, that the state constitution's requirement that voters approve all general revenue bond issues would not apply to bonds issued to build a prison. This holding was based on two considerations: first, voters would never approve a bond issue to build a prison; and second, our current prison did not meet federal standards under the U.S. Constitution's Eighth Amendment.

The conclusion that voter approval was not necessary for issuance of bonds to build a prison followed from something known as the supremacy doctrine: Federal law supercedes all conflicting state law, and the limitation on bond issues, requiring, as it does, voter approval, would inevitably prevent the state from meeting federal prison standards. A more conservative judicial approach would have been simply to order the prison closed on a particular date and let the executive branch and the voters sort the problem out as best they could. However, practical experience instructed the court that when the date for closing came, there would be no facility to receive the prisoners, and we would be confronted with a choice between backing down or releasing murderers, rapists and robbers upon an unsuspecting world.

erally run down the neighborhood. The furlough and work-release programs that captured the voters' imagination in the 1988 presidential campaign are almost exclusively the result of budget pressures and community resistance rather than woolly-headed liberals or weak-kneed judges.

As Richard B. Abell, assistant U. S. attorney general in charge of the Office of Justice Programs, recently wrote:

> Two good ideas—fiscal conservatism and getting tough with criminals—are on a collision course. Responding to public outrage about crime and to the realization that criminal rehabilitation usually doesn't work, state legislatures have been enacting tougher sentencing practices for repeat offenders. The legislators want to eliminate revolving-door justice, to redefine "life sentence" as more than parole in three to five years. But these worthy goals are threatened by prison crowding and the reluctance of taxpayers to appropriate scarce resources for new prison construction and rehabilitation of old facilities.[9]

In West Virginia, a state with cheap land and reasonable wage rates, we have designed a new prison to house 1,023 inmates divided between medium and maximum security. At the planning stage (when everyone is optimistic) the estimated cost per bed is $44,000. Elsewhere, particularly in the urban states, it costs between $50,000 and $100,000 to provide a new prison bed. But that's just the beginning of the cost: Prisoners must be fed, given adequate medical treatment, educated, provided with chaplains, guarded, educated and otherwise cared for. That means that the yearly cost per adult inmate in a new prison is between

[9]R. B. Abell, "Beyond Willie Horton," *Policy Review*, Winter 1989, p.32.

$25,000 and $50,000.[10] The exact cost between those two rough numbers depends upon how optimistic one is about the opportunities for rehabilitation. The greater the extent to which authorities make a serious effort to educate and counsel their charges, the higher the cost.

In general, most prison systems are not very optimistic about maximum-security adult prisoners. But nearly all systems are reasonably optimistic about delinquent adolescents. Here, however, the costs become astronomical. In West Virginia, our one good school for aggressive, disturbed male offenders between fourteen and eighteen years old costs $154 per day per child. At that particular school, which has an average daily census of 39.2 inmates, there are 84 full-time staff members, many of whom are high-wage professional teachers, counselors or psychologists.

The lines I quoted above from Richard Abell are from a long article by him that elicited strong reaction, both pro and con. I found that this article, along with the responses it elicited, gives a thumbnail summary of the current debate throughout the United States about incarceration. In the article, Mr. Abell directs our attention to a Rand Corporation survey of 2,190 criminals in three states. The survey found that career burglars averaged between 76 and 118 burglaries per year. Lesser larcenists, such as shoplifters and pickpockets, averaged between 135 and 202 thefts per year. Ten percent of offenders committed over 600 crimes per year, while about half the Rand Corporation's sample committed fewer than 15 crimes per year. Thus, in the Rand study, the overall average of all crimes committed per criminal per year ranged between 187 and 287.

Mr. Abell then invites us to do some simple arithmetic and combine it with a little common sense. Multiplying the average

---

[10]Currently in West Virginia, using a prison built right after the Civil War, it still costs us $11,500 out-of-pocket cash to house a prisoner for a year.

cost of crime ($2,300) by the average number of offenses (187, the low end of the range), we should find that a typical offender in the survey is responsible for $430,000 annually in crime costs. The cost to imprison the same offender for one year is $25,000 (also the low end of the range), which means that a year of crime is more costly to society by a factor of 17 to 1 than imprisonment. Furthermore, this takes into consideration only the out-of-pocket money costs. It does not take into consideration pain and suffering, the cost of taking precautions to avoid victimization and the annoyance of reporting crime, applying for insurance and testifying in court.

Mr. Abell's strident article prompted a rash of letters from highly respected professionals in sociology, political science and criminal justice. Many of the critical letters pointed out serious flaws in the Rand Corporation's methodology. John J. DiIulio, Jr.—a Harvard-trained Ph.D. and professor of politics and public affairs at Princeton University—admitted that there were good reasons to be less than overwhelmed by the statistical majesty of Rand's number crunchers. Nonetheless, Professor DiIulio argued, even if we cut the Rand survey's results in half, imprisonment would still be cheaper by a factor of more than 8 to 1![11]

The prison reformers, however, entirely discounted the Rand survey's relevance and denied that cost:benefit analysis can be applied appropriately to incarceration. Thus, Samuel Walker, Professor of Criminal Justice at the University of Nebraska, argued:

> Ah, but what if we lock up only the truly
> high-rate offenders? This runs afoul of the
> "prediction problem." There is a vast body of
> research (summarized in my book *Sense and
> Nonsense About Crime*), which argues that we

[11]Letter to the Editor, *Policy Review*, Spring 1989, p. 89.

do not have the diagnostic tools to identify
that select group from among all convicted
offenders . . .

The net result is that we will incarcerate
many more low-rate offenders (15 or fewer
crimes per year). The "savings" will only be
8 percent of what Mr. Abell promises . . .

A more realistic analysis of Mr. Abell's
data yields a very different result. The
typical offender commits 15 or fewer crimes
per year; more than half of all felonies are
thefts; the most expensive category of thefts
involves an average of $646 in stolen
property. The annual "savings" is $9,690.
Let's be generous and double it, for the sake
of argument. This is still less than the
annual cost of imprisonment.[12]

Professor Walker was temperate in his criticism, and his
methodology was at least as serious as Mr. Abell's, the Rand
Corporation's and Professor DiIulio's. However, another commentator probably speaks for a larger group of social science
professionals in the contemptuous way he dismisses any effort
to establish cost:benefit criteria in prison construction and criminal sentencing. Jerome G. Miller, an official with the National
Center on Institutions and Alternatives in Alexandria, Virginia,
writes:

If [Abell] is right, . . . we'd be well on
the way to erasing the federal deficit,
widening the safety net, and putting SDI in
orbit simply by doubling the number of
inmates in our prisons and jails . . .

The image that comes to mind is that of a
studious Robert McNamara milling over

[12]*Ibid*, p. 90.

computer print-outs of "body-counts," running
them through his computer, and concluding we
were winning the Vietnam war. It's a formula
for similar disaster in our "war" against crime.[13]

The interesting aspect of the dialogue provoked by Mr. Abell's article is not who is right, but rather that the same dialogue has been going on for an entire lifetime without ever leading to any firm policy consensus. Each new generation of social scientists has its well-intentioned prison reformers and its hard liners: I can only conclude that where you come out in this prison business in terms of practical suggestions is roughly where you came in ideologically. Deeply entrenched convictions are never altered by the facts.

Indeed, if those full of the milk of human kindness could finally achieve a broad consensus that we must attack the root causes of crime and load the underclass up with heavy doses of social services, jobs, training and intensely supervised probation, the crime rate would probably fall precipitously, although taxes would increase. Nonetheless, even with the tax increases there would still be a net economic gain, but not necessarily to those who pay the taxes.

Alternatively, if the hard liners could achieve a consensus, we could build enormous prisons in isolated areas and construct the twentieth-century equivalent of medieval *oubliettes*, into which prisoners were thrown simply to be forgotten. This would also entail substantial expense, but the crime rate would drop precipitously. As Mr. Abell's article, the Rand Corporation's survey and the criticism from respected professionals amply demonstrate, however, there is no consensus at all. And this is exactly the point of my digression into the debate on prison reform: that *absolutely nothing* will be done except traditional muddling

[13]*Ibid.*

125

through, which implies that the crime rate will continue to soar. Although we won't pay big taxes (because no one can agree on how to spend the crime-control money) we'll continue to pay through the nose in lost property, lost time, personal injuries, private security costs and, occasionally, with our lives.

This is not a book about crime, but rather a book about acceptable citizen responses to crime. Remember, the social liberals (for want of a better label) decry both the privatization of space *and* community law enforcement—particularly community patrolling. Somehow public enforcement is seen as better—more democratic, less subject to vigilante abuses, less discriminatory because it doesn't narrow the spaces available for poor people to roam, etc., etc. The question, of course, is where a workable system of *public* enforcement is going to come from in our lifetime? The answer is that a workable system of public enforcement will never emerge because of our lack of political consensus. But if it is not possible to achieve a political consensus in a large, diverse political community such as a city or a state, it may yet be possible to achieve such a consensus in a small, homogenous community such as a neighborhood. At that micro-level it is possible to see direct correlations between reduction in the crime rate and specific activities on a narrow front, which is what community patrolling, community intervention with high risk groups like adolescents, and the widespread privatization of space are all about.

The reader who bought this book because he or she now mirrors the attitude of the crowds in Paddy Chayevsky's movie *Network*, who yelled, "I'm mad as hell and I'm not going to take it any more!" probably wonders how the political process can be as insensitive as it is to crime control when we are all scared to death. The answer to this question requires an explanation of many of the counterintuitive practical features of Congress and state legislatures. Once the reader understands the mechanics of his or her own legislature, the paralysing effect of the lack of consensus that I have described in this chapter and the previous one will, perhaps, make more sense. But even more important, I may succeed in rounding out a convincing case for the proposition that we must begin to use self-help in crime control because the government both cannot and will not protect us under any circumstances conceivable in the real political world.

The active person who is always impatient to get to the bottom line—in this case, how to take back his or her neighborhood—may find the next six pages or so that describe a legislature boring. But what I hope to do here is provide necessary ammunition so that advocates of community patrolling and privatization of space can confront their critics and detractors on equal terms. The central thesis of this book is that public-sector law enforcement is failing miserably, so we must go back to defending ourselves. When we defend ourselves, however, abuses are inevitable, so modern-day vigilantes will be in for some rough public criticism, much of it from skilled media professionals and well-trained professors.

But in the final analysis, all of the criticism that I anticipate will amount to nothing more than a comparison between some *ideal* public enforcement system and a *real* vigilante system. It is at this point that the proponents of modern-day vigilantism need to be able to cite the details of how the real political system works in order to force the discussion into a comparison between a real vigilante system and a real public enforcement system. In Chapter 3 I explained the hidden agendas of numerous powerful political interests because an understanding of those agendas is indispensable to an understanding of why the real public enforcement system will always fail. The final bit of practical politics that the proponents of modern-day vigilantism must master is the rough outline of how a legislature works. Once the reader can combine the hidden agendas of those who would undermine the enforcement system with the mechanics of a legislature, the reader will be able to formulate an iron-clad case for community self-policing.

The legislative branch of government, contrary to popular belief, is not in business to pass good laws. In fact, it is fair to say, ultimately without the least derision, that the legislative branch is an institution designed to do nothing. In that characterization, the emphasis is not on "do nothing" but rather on "designed." American government is preeminently characterized by a system of measured straining in opposite directions. In this system of calculated, self-correcting checks and balances, a conservative force straining toward inertia is a legitimate and necessary component. This is exactly the function for which a legislature was designed.

When describing a legislature, the word "conservative" does not imply a reactionary force driven by the selfish interests of the propertied class, but rather just the maintenance of the *status quo*, even if the *status quo* is at the moment an elaborate scheme to redistribute wealth. My ultimate conclusion about the legislative branch is close to Trollope's conclusion about one of his more interesting female characters in *The Way We Live Now*: "The woman was false from head to foot, but there was much good in her, false though she was."

In any given congressional or state legislative session, the number of petitions for changes in the law favoring special interests are countless. Labor unions want new rules permitting third-party boycotts to strengthen their bargaining position during strikes; manufacturers want "right to work" laws that make union membership as a condition of employment illegal; junk mailers want lower postal rates; miners and loggers want greater access to public lands; environmental groups want more stringent pollution control even at the cost of jobs; huge American companies like Boeing, which need foreign sales to underwrite their fixed costs, want a larger budget for the Export-Import Bank; lawyers want more money for the Legal Services Corporation; and state teacher unions and the American Federation of Teachers want greater federal subsidies to state education and higher salaries for teachers. Everyone has a wish list as long as your arm, and each group stays up late designing ways to do in its enemies.

Furthermore, all of these groups represent substantial numbers of voters or campaign contributors who have legitimate demands on the political process. The question becomes how individual elected legislators can say no to the host of predatory vested interests trying to do in the average unorganized taxpayer or consumer, without losing the next election. It is at this point that the genius of the legislative design enters the picture. Because the machinery of a legislature is *designed* to do nothing, legislators can rest easy, secure in the knowledge that almost all predatory legislation will die a natural death through the operation of the complex and cumbersome legislative process itself. Furthermore, if the legislative machinery works as it was designed and intended, the happy demise of very bad predatory legislation will occur without anyone's being *on record* as voting against specific special-interest bills. Bad legislation simply dies in committee or gets amended to such an extent that its own supporters order its destruction. And that, in turn, is good for legislators' job security.

The structure of the bicameral federal and state legislatures didn't just spring from the minds of the Founding Fathers. The legislative branch is in no way "modern," nor is it even a modern reconstruction of a classical ideal. Both congress and our state legislatures are copies of an English feudal institution, namely parliament, which evolved over six-hundred-odd years. In its original feudal form, the English parliament was an institution designed, in the strongest possible sense, to do nothing. Parliament emerged from a deep-seated desire of upper-class English landowners to curtail, as far as possible, the king's ability to levy taxes or change the traditional customs and usages of the realm. Medieval English parliaments were expected to preserve the delicate balance of power between a central authority on the one hand and local clergy and landowners on the other. Any redistribution of power in favor of the central authority was anathema to local lords because such a shift would allow those in control of central government to skim economic benefits off the top for themselves, their friends and their kin, leaving less to be skimmed off by the powerful local folk. Parliament's defeat, then, of Sir Robert Peel's proposed national police force, discussed in Chapter 1, was entirely in keeping with what parliament had been doing *vis à vis* the central government for five hundred years and is an excellent historical example of how the legislative body will usually quash any excursions into new and different ways of dealing with society's problems.

In the middle ages, taxation had little to do with redistribution of wealth from rich to poor. Public works were limited, and in England enhanced military expenditures were almost always of an offensive rather than a defensive nature. The king was constantly seeking instant influxes of money to finance his grandiose foreign adventures—like the wars in France to which I have alluded in Chapters 1 and 3—or to underwrite his friends' and retainers' life-styles. Naturally, private subjects were reluctant to pay. Therefore, resistance to the central government was essential to the preservation of a life worth living, and so in bygone days the notion of a conservative force in government had a far stronger attraction as a philosophical principle than perhaps it has today.

The point is that parliaments came into being not to initiate change but to prevent it, and that is largely what they still do today. It was not by accident that the war cry of English parliamentary leaders during the twelfth and thirteenth centuries was *nolumus leges anglicae mutare* —traditionally translated as ''the laws of England shall never change!'' Here we have an express commitment to the *status quo* in the strongest possible terms.

Although the democratic liturgy would have it otherwise, most people are at heart conservative; certainly most people fear any change in the legal or social structure that might threaten their job security or economic welfare. Everyone, of course, wants change that is in the "public interest," but people cannot agree on what the public interest is. The debate among the experts on the costs and benefits of prisons is a good example. Mr. Abell sees the public interest as locking everyone up and throwing away the key; Mr. Miller sees it as pumping the whole "peace dividend" into social projects designed to uplift the underclass both socially and economically.

Here we must recall for a moment the point that I made at the beginning of the chapter: The people most frequently victimized by crime pay the lowest taxes. Large tax increases to support public law enforcement—more police, more prisons, more social services, alternatives to incarceration, juvenile schools and mental hospitals—are simply one of many available schemes to redistribute wealth from rich to poor. Legislatures, however, are designed to be bastions against such wealth redistributions and so they can hardly be expected to create legislation that will increase the official government response to crime.

Because the maintenance of the *status quo* is, on balance, the most generally acceptable result that a legislature can yield to the community as a whole, all legislative machinery is designed to advance that end. First of all, it is necessary for any bill to be passed by both houses *in exactly the same form*. That constitutional requirement is hardly a device tending toward the rapid passage of controversial legislation. And the requirement that bills pass both houses is a conscious part of the design of a legislature that helps insure that legislation without broad support will die a natural death.

In England, during the civil war of the 1640s, there was a

point at which the House of Commons took over all legislative functions. However, at that moment the House of Commons' performance became so corrupt and venal (in terms of passing self-serving special-interest legislation) that the House of Lords was gleefully restored to its former prominence at Charles II's restoration in 1660. Even today, in the face of its militantly meritocratic, anti-aristocratic political philosophy, England retains a House of Lords with delaying powers so that there can be an appeal, as it were, from the people drunk to the people sober. In England, in order for legislation to pass quickly, that legislation must be approved by the House of Lords. After World War II, Norway established a unicameral parliament, but the results were so perverse that the single house voluntarily divided itself into two chambers and, by internal rule, required bills to be approved independently by both units before becoming law.

Legislative procedures are consciously designed to permit the silent death of divisive legislation without anyone's being on record as opposing it. Thus a member can introduce a truly rapacious bill and be confident that the speaker will assign it to a committee that meets infrequently and will never get around to considering it, or that the chairman of an important and diligent committee will never place the bill on the agenda, or that the rules committee will never allow the bill to come to the floor for a vote.

Although the abjectly venal and self-serving nature of government has changed since the early parliaments, many other things have not changed at all. Of these, the most important is that when powerful interests come to the government seeking a change in the law, their intentions are almost always predatory. The difference between general-interest legislation and special-interest legislation is usually difficult to find; even the bills that appear to be most in the general interest are urged by individuals or institutions that have special interests in their passage. For example, most bills designed to further education are sponsored by teachers and administrators, not by parents and children. Improved education is obviously in the public interest, yet it is even more in the private interest of educators. Better education implies higher teacher salaries, smaller classes, better working conditions, larger travel budgets and greater personal prestige for teachers.

The same observation about self-seeking motives among those urging government programs in education can be made about those urging government programs in crime control. Everyone wants crime-control money—police for enforcement, corrections departments for prisons, social service agencies for juvenile shelters and other protective services, probation departments for incarceration alternatives, and private companies or nonprofit organizations for hare-brained schemes ranging from private prisons to sending convicted felons to Harvard. Lack of consensus, then, has a self-interested as well as a principled side—a problem legislatures usually handle by doing nothing.

Naive as I was in my young political days, I was always dumbfounded by the proportion of time in a legislature devoted to sorting out special-interest legislation versus improving the commonweal. But the way things are done makes perfect sense given practical reality: Special-interest constituencies are organized and can deliver publicity, votes and campaign contributions to elected officeholders. The most powerful lobby in West Virginia, for example, is the teachers' union. In any legislative session the most intensely considered piece of legislation is the package that includes a salary increase for teachers. Furthermore, this package often becomes the cynosure around which other trades and bargains are struck.

When teachers get a raise, that percentage increase sets the pattern for all other state employees, and ultimately leads either to increased taxes or to the diversion of money from other programs, like prisons or computers for the public schools. Although citizens are seriously concerned about crime control, there is no organized single-issue lobby demanding money, urging programs, exacting compromises and threatening dire consequences to legislators who won't cooperate. That is why, notwithstanding media preoccupation with crime and delinquency, no significant improvement in crime control ever emerges from a state legislature. Who is out there, like the teachers, demanding construction of new prisons, and backing up their demands with campaign contributions and militant election-day organizations? Who is willing to organize pickets and demonstrations when criminals like Willie Horton are put back on the street because of a shortage of cells? The answer is no one.

The closest thing I have ever seen to a real crime-control lobby is MADD, "Mothers Against Drunk Drivers." This national citizen group, founded and staffed primarily by relatives of those killed by drunk drivers, has had a significant effect on enforcing highway sobriety. The organization began in the 1970s in response to our cavalier tolerance of people, usually men, who have had one too many and then kill our children on the highways. The success of MADD depended, however, upon two major factors that are seldom found in law enforcement projects: First, what MADD wanted, namely a severe tightening of the drunk-driving laws with quickly processed, mandatory administrative revocation of licenses, didn't cost any money. Second, everyone in MADD, and all those who supported them, agreed on the program, namely getting drunks off the road.

The intentionally conservative nature of a legislature aids and abets all of the low-visibility special interests that I described in Chapter 3 who, for one reason or another, want to gut some particular piece of the law enforcement apparatus. The insurance industry, which wants clogged court calendars, will have legislative allies who are committee chairmen; the vice lords, who want limited enforcement of the gambling, drinking and drug laws, will have allies who are committee chairmen;[14] and a lot of members both in the leadership and on the back benches are always reluctant to raise the level of police harassment by creating more officers.

Therefore, one potentially constructive offshoot of volunteer community crime control may be the development of a political nucleus around which serious programs for expanded public enforcement can be initiated and implemented. A big part of that program will probably be highly cost-effective government help for community patrols and other community anticrime activities.

I have dwelled at this length on the nature of legislatures simply to point out how nearly impossible the task of making major strides in public law enforcement really is. Even militant, well-organized single-issue lobbies like a state teachers' union can't get much money out of a state legislature—indeed, teachers aren't very well paid anywhere. And, as I explained in Chapter 3, there are many people who are strongly against violent crime, but are even more strongly against some piece of the public machinery (such as more police) necessary to deal with violent crime. Given the structure of a legislature, it should by now be obvious that it is much easier to *kill* a bill than it is to pass one. Although passing a bill requires enthusiastic support from the leadership of two entirely independent chambers, along with at least passive support from the back bench members, killing a bill requires only the animosity of one powerful committee chairman, a speaker, a senate president or about seven members of a rules committee.

As I review the academic literature on private security, com-

---

[14]This proposition became painfully clear on 14 February 1990 when Washington's mayor, Marion Barry, was indicted by a federal grand jury for a number of drug-related offenses after being caught red-handed using drugs. Apparently the mayor was deeply involved with Washington's vice lords. If such a close alliance between a mayor (who must appreciate at some level that he lives in a glass house) and the underworld can exist for years, how much more likely is a similar relationship to arise between a low-visibility legislative committee chairman and the underworld?

munity patrolling and privatization of space, the proposition keeps recurring in myriad forms that somehow private action to protect ourselves is selfish and immoral. In essence, the argument runs something like this: Certain favored groups—the rich who can afford private security, residents of middle-class planned communities who can limit access to their areas and ethnically homogeneous (mainly white) owners of houses in the suburbs— can protect themselves, but this happens at the expense of communal efforts that would otherwise be available to everyone. Therefore, it is supposed, because those with political power and the money to pay taxes can take measures to protect themselves, those favored few opt out of the public enforcement system, leaving that system under-funded, under-staffed, and under-supported politically. Consequently, if the favored few won't pay the taxes for a public enforcement system, the favored few should be punished by not being allowed to have private security.

In this argument, then, a false linkage is formed: It is concluded that because the rich who live in Palm Beach or Kiawah Island have figured out a system to protect themselves, the slums of Miami, Chicago and Los Angeles are dangerous places to live. But this chain of reasoning is entirely fallacious. Miserable law enforcement is a serious problem, but miserable law enforcement is only one of hundreds of problems any legislature faces. How about miserable schools, miserable public hospitals and miserable public housing? People try to protect themselves from crime because nothing can be done about the breakdown of the public safety system. Nobody but a "cop nut" enjoys enforcing the law himself; therefore, resorting to private and community measures—very slow as they have been in coming—is dictated only by practical necessity.

Perhaps one analogy is in order. In the big Northeastern cities like New York and Washington, it is a rare family with an income over $60,000 a year that uses the public schools. Everywhere in the Northeast there are private schools, and many of them, like the Catholic schools, are subsidized by charities and are therefore cheap and readily available to all who are willing to abide by their rules. Unless a student is lucky enough to go to one of the outstanding magnet schools available in the public system (Bronx High School of Science in New York or Duke Ellington High School for the Performing Arts in Washington, for example), ambitious parents will stretch themselves to avoid the public school system. This is simply because the public school system can't be made to work acceptably from the point of view of ambitious middle-class parents (or those who wish their children to join the middle class) in the cities. The typical inner-city school cannot prepare a student for Harvard or MIT.

But elsewhere, like Charleston, West Virginia, the public education system works superbly. In Charleston, except for a few small Catholic schools and a few evangelical protestant ones, there are no private schools. The entire upper-middle class gleefully uses the public system, at least up to the ninth grade, in spite of the fact that the upper-middle class in Charleston has far more disposable income (because of our low cost of living) than the upper-middle class has in either New York or Washington. Furthermore, the upper-middle class in America's heartland has come out of the exact same schools as the upper-middle class in the cities. Many went to state universities, but many also went to private prep schools, Ivy League colleges and fine private universities. When the public system can be made to work, the prosperous in the United States are happy to use and support it. But resorting to private means when the public system is not working is neither selfish nor snobbish; it is simple self-defense in an entirely hopeless situation.

To carry the school example one step further, resorting to private schools has been the salvation of the honest, ambitious poor in the cities as well. Catholic schools, while ostensibly private, have a long tradition of educating impoverished Catholic immigrants. Consequently, Catholic schools in the cities try to charge only what poor, struggling families can afford, which often means nothing. The Catholic schools are fully integrated racially, and although the Catholic schools' social class mix is probably slightly higher than the typical public school, the difference is marginal in terms of income. It is substantial, however, in terms of values and attitudes.

What makes the Catholic schools overwhelmingly superior to their public sector counterparts? It probably is the bare fact that they are *private*. Every student who attends a Catholic school does so because either the student or his parents *want* him to be there. Consequently, there are no serious discipline problems, little drug dealing and little disruption by one group of the learning opportunities for other groups. Why? Because anyone who causes trouble is out. Many argue, then, that the public system is left with all the misfits, troublemakers and children born to unwed mothers on drugs who will never send their children even to a free private school. That's true, but in schools, as in crime control, it makes greater sense to *expand* the private sector to be more inclusive than to beat our heads against the stone wall of politics to try to make the public sector work.

Chapter V

WHAT WORKS, WHAT DOESN'T

Before a person can be wholeheartedly in favor of community policing, he must have at least as much faith in the ordinary citizen as he does in government authorities. Serious literature, popular folklore, television plays and movies usually portray the community of ordinary citizens as villains and some lonely individual as the hero. Thus we have the lynch mob of "The Ox Bow Incident" and the narrow-mindedness of the Harper Valley P.T.A. Writers like Sinclair Lewis made careers bashing the middle class, and in the 1950s books like Vance Packard's *The Crack In The Picture Window* appeared to decry the conformity and lack of taste of suburban America. In turn, all of this is reinforced by our own quarrels with those around us—neighbors, workmates, employers, school authorities and those with whom we are forced to do business.

Yet the overall quality of the American people is a wonder to behold. Once as a student I was driving across the country when my car developed a serious oil leak in La Crosse, Wisconsin. It was a Saturday night, there was a blinding rain storm and the mechanic in the gas station said that I would need to wait until Monday morning to get the car fixed. A stranger happened in to make a phone call and, seeing me distraught, asked what the problem was. He looked at the defective part, averred that he could fix it in ten minutes and then proceeded to cut a new gasket from a piece of light cardboard box. It worked perfectly, and I went on to California. I never knew the man's name, but I have always remembered that he took ten minutes out of his life to help me for no better reason than that he knew something that I didn't.

Local organizations such as parent-teacher associations, the United Fund, churches, the Jaycees, Rotary, Lions Club and National Ski Patrol perform important functions in our communal lives. Although there are a lot of disagreeable and even downright bad people out there, when a person is in trouble and encounters a stranger, that stranger is more likely to behave like my man in La Crosse, Wisconsin, than he is to be unpleasant. Furthermore, some organizational settings tend to bring out the best in people. One such setting is a jury, where six or twelve strangers cooperate—sometimes for a long time—to decide a case of enormous importance to the litigants. Volunteer fire departments are a superb feature of rural American life. Big fires are dangerous, and every year there are feats of heroism by unpaid firemen who risk their lives to save people, animals and property.

The pervasive reservations that exist about community policing must emerge from something other than lack of faith in the general competence and good intentions of American volunteers. Indeed, there are major differences between policing and all the other activities that American volunteers perform so successfully. Any form of policing carries with it the opportunity for petty individual power that will inevitably attract a lunatic fringe that is not attracted to membership in a P.T.A., church, Lions Club, volunteer fire department or even a jury.

Policemen have implied authority to tell other people what to do, and that type of individual authority brings out of the woodwork a surplus of not-so-bright, insecure, mentally unstable persons who lust after power. Anyone who has been around police departments knows that there are "cop nuts" who have always wanted to be policemen but have failed the civil service exams. These unfortunate souls hang around police stations and vicariously satisfy their personal drives for power and authority by associating with the officers they perceive as power figures.

These observations lead us to the first conclusion about what doesn't work in any system of community patrolling—namely, guns. Certainly guns are not an inherent feature of high-quality patrolling, because the English police on neighborhood foot patrol, who are renowned for their competence, do not carry guns. Indeed, in any volunteer patrol group, it cannot be emphasized enough that guns are extremely dangerous, even when in the hands of people trained to use them.

Regular police officers usually go through a police academy that lasts many months, where much of their training is in the use of firearms. During this training regular police are taught not only how to maintain and shoot their weapons, but when *not* to shoot. I had a lot of experience with weapons as an army captain in Vietnam because I was surrounded for a year by men who all carried one or two weapons about their persons at all times. In those days my biggest concern was that boys eighteen to twenty-four years old would shoot me or one another through negligence, fear or simple mistake.[1] Furthermore, it takes simulated combat

---

[1] During the Tet offensive of 1969 I lived in a small compound in the city of Bien Hoa. In the event of an attack, I commanded three bunkers, two of which were on the perimeter and the third directly behind as a reserve position (the classic two up and one back.) We would scramble into a defensive position in the bunkers, weapons at the ready, at the first sign of an attack anywhere in the Bien Hoa area. On these

experience to understand how a .38 or .45 caliber bullet ricochets, and how much solid material is required to stop such a bullet. When confronted by an armed criminal, the best defense is retreat; certainly capturing criminals is not worth risking the lives of innocent passersby who might get caught in a crossfire.

Of the roughly 1.4 million private security guards in the United States, a small percentage are armed. Those who are armed are usually off-duty policemen (hired to patrol private areas, and wearing their official uniforms), bank guards, railroad detectives and trained personnel who patrol well-fenced private areas where there can be no mistake about the reason an intruder is on the property. Private security guards patrolling public spaces like shopping malls, parking lots, office buildings and night clubs are hardly ever armed. This simply reflects the fact that the likelihood of injury to bystanders, low-level unarmed criminals and even the guards themselves far outweighs any advantage that might proceed from giving the guards added authority or better defense.

James Q. Wilson, who is probably America's leading authority on police patrolling, has concluded, after reviewing all of the published studies on the subject, that what makes the police effective in maintaining order and reducing crime (as opposed

---

occasions I usually spent my time running from bunker to bunker yelling at the green garrison troops that I would court martial the first man who put a round in his chamber before my command. I would actually demand to see all rifles, M79s, grease guns and other weapons with open breeches because I was terrified that my trigger-happy kids would shoot one of our own returning patrols (who frequently dressed in the same black pajamas as the Viet Cong) or would inadvertently shoot one another inside the bunker. My biggest fear, however, was that the men in the reserve bunker would open fire and shoot the men in the forward bunkers in the back.

I always carried a Colt .45, but unless I was in an area where there was a fire fight in progress, I never put a magazine in the weapon, because I was afraid I'd shoot myself. It seemed to me that if I had time to draw the pistol, I'd also have time to load it, all of which took an extra two seconds—*at most*. In a war there are far more casualties from friendly fire than the army ever admits publicly: No mother wants to believe that her son was killed by some inattentive fellow soldier who was cleaning a weapon, or that her son was shot by his mate as he came back from patrol.

to apprehending felons after the fact) is the mere presence of a uniformed policeman. Psychologists, he reports, have done many studies on why people fail to stop crimes in progress or to assist persons being attacked, and these researchers have concluded that the cause is not "apathy" or "selfishness" but rather the absence of plausible grounds for intervening in someone else's dispute. Furthermore, the problem becomes more acute when there are many people around; the very existence of a large number of spectators reduces any one person's authority to intervene on behalf of the people as a whole. The police officer's uniform, however, singles him out as a person who *must* accept responsibility if asked, and officers are expected to be more evenhanded and objective than an ordinary citizen who has no training in the law.[2]

Therefore, most of what can be accomplished in a neighborhood by an armed officer can also be accomplished by an unarmed one. What is far more important than a firearm, however, is that patrol members be clearly identified as persons responsible for law enforcement. In this regard, it is important to wear some distinguishing attire, like the red beret and distinctive T-shirt of the Guardian Angels, or even the standard police uniform worn by most private security guards.

My own choice for distinctive attire, in a neighborhood where participants can afford such clothes, is a scarlet coat like the ones worn by the Canadian Northwest Mounted Police. A uniform like that can be identified immediately from afar, but it is probably far too elaborate for the ordinary citizen to want to maintain. American state police always have more elaborate uniforms than local police, and state policemen usually wear the distinctive campaign hat worn by drill sergeants in the military to distinguish them from local police. The F.B.I., on the other

[2]James Q. Wilson, *Thinking About Crime*, Basic Books (rev'd. ed., New York, 1983), p. 88.

hand, who do no preventive patrolling, wear no uniforms at all unless they contemplate an arrest (including, possibly, a shoot-out), at which point they put on distinctive jackets that clearly say F.B.I. so that they won't shoot one another.

When it comes to exclusively defensive weapons, like billy clubs and the chemical compound "Mace," however, there are few reliable general guidelines. Many private security guards do carry some type of defensive weapon—particularly billy clubs— but the most valuable contribution of these devices is probably that, like a uniform and badge, they give the appearance of authority.[3] In many states, like New York, carrying any type of weapon without a license is a criminal offense; in others, like West Virginia, Vermont and Texas, all weapons, including fire-arms, may be carried openly without violating the law. The English bobbies carry night sticks on patrol. The Guardian An-gels, on the other hand, and many security guards, carry no weapons at all, while other security guards in public places carry night sticks and Mace, so there appears to be no consensus.

Companies (and their insurers) concerned with potential lia-bility for assault and battery by their security guards appear to have no hard and fast rules about defensive weapons. It seems to be a matter of what works. In places where people are likely to become rowdy, drunk and violent, like shopping malls, park-ing lots and rock concerts, defensive weapons seem to be prev-alent among private guards, while in office buildings and hotels they are not.

Volunteers, however, do not have the ability to enforce the

[3]In the army, every compound on a base has a staff duty officer during the nighttime hours. The job of staff duty officer rotates among the young subalterns who sit by the phone, react to problems, check guard posts and generally supervise the troops living in the area. Traditionally, the staff duty officer wears a pistol belt with a standard issue holster for a Colt .45; however, there is seldom a pistol in the holster. The holster is simply a symbol of authority. The army is smart enough to know that unless an officer is responsible for the gold at Fort Knox or the keys to nuclear weapons, it's stupid to entrust an inexperienced kid with a loaded weapon!

law through the use of force, except to the extent that they can intervene successfully to thwart crimes, like rape, that are in progress. Night sticks and Mace may be valuable in an altercation that gets out of hand, but when it appears that attempted apprehension or the quelling of rowdy behavior will inevitably lead to violence, the official police must be summoned. This means that the most valuable protection for volunteers are two-way radios linked either directly to the police or to a volunteer dispatcher whose job it is to summon official aid through the regular telephone network, perhaps using a special number that insures an immediate response. If it becomes common knowledge that volunteers will be assisted immediately by the police, the need to call the police will arise less frequently.

But this is not to say that our volunteers are nothing but glorified police call boxes. Rowdy teenagers will usually respond positively to adult authority, and studies conclusively show that muggers, purse snatchers and other petty thieves are significantly deterred by the presence of patrols—either the police, private security or the Guardian Angels. This is partially because a person with a uniform and a badge can rally the support of another law-abiding citizen to assist him in stopping an assault, preventing a rape or apprehending a mugger.

On another level, in a residential neighborhood, simply having obvious vigilance deters burglars and car thieves. Such a simple expedient as following a pick-up truck at 2:00 A.M. discourages a would-be burglar from stopping in the patrolled area, because inevitably the patrol will have recorded the license number and written down a description of the truck. It takes several minutes for a car thief to enter and start a parked car; regular patrols, then, particularly if they are equipped with search lights, will discourage thieves from attempting car theft. Furthermore, much of the most annoying street crime comes from teenage vandals who simply enjoy puncturing tires and doing other types of gratuitous damage. Patrols with lights, cameras and a knowledge

145

of the neighborhood can prevent such vandalism as is committed by bored youngsters traveling in packs. Obviously, the juvenile gangs of Los Angeles or Chicago that I described in Chapter 2 who are armed with Uzis and AK-47s will not respond to adult authority, but the normal pack of teenagers who do not rise to the level of a professional criminal gang can usually be controlled.

It is far more important for volunteers to be equipped with uniforms, radios, still cameras, note pads and video cameras than weapons of any sort. Furthermore, insisting on evidence collection and preventive measures in the patrol function will go a long way toward keeping the cop nuts out of an otherwise respectable community police force. To the extent that defensive weapons short of firearms are demanded (and knowing the macho of the average American male that seems inevitable) training should emphasize that weapons are primarily useful as symbols of community authority, and for defensive purposes only as a last resort. No one should be associated with any community organization that allows its members to carry firearms.

The essence of community law enforcement is enforcing the standards of the community within that community and keeping out strangers who are up to no good. The civil rights movement of the 1960s had the effect of severely limiting the discretion of police officers, because the low-level misdemeanors like vagrancy, public drunkenness, and being a suspicious person had made it easy for the official police to exclude undesirable strangers from the areas they patrolled. "Vagrancy" was usually defined as having no visible means of support, and "being a suspicious person" would cover driving a pickup truck in a residential neighborhood at 2:00 A.M. without being able to give a good reason. The courts struck down laws against vagrancy and being a suspicious person for reasons that made a great deal of sense in the 1960s; with 20/20 hindsight, however, we can now see that notwithstanding these laws' potential for abuse, they nonetheless served a legitimate crime-control purpose.[4]

The role of the police is to enforce the values of the community *in* the community. Laws against vagrancy, drunkenness and being a suspicious person allowed the police to interrogate strangers, determine their intentions and then move them on under threat of arrest. But the standards that were enforced were different depending on the community involved. Thus, in a neighborhood full of old houses cut up into apartments rented to college students, there was a higher tolerance for loud and rowdy behavior than in an adjoining neighborhood of middle-aged couples. In the cities, each neighborhood had its own distinctive ethnic, class, racial, and cultural qualities, so the code of behavior that was enforced differed from neighborhood to neighborhood.[5]

In general, communities coalesce around those in the community with middle-class values. In a homogeneous community, it is the ministers, teachers, merchants, doctors and property owners who are the natural leaders. The comparatively low crime rate in the United States in the first sixty years of this century reflected the fact that most people lived in cohesive communities with identifiable standards.[6] Then two things happened: First, a combination of the automobile and good roads on which to drive opened up large areas outside the cities where urban workers

[4]I am not being critical of the U.S. Supreme Court's rulings on these laws. Elsewhere I have discussed how striking down statutes of this sort was necessary to enhance labor mobility, job opportunities and equal access to public accommodations. *See*, R. Neely, *How Courts Govern America*, Yale University Press (New Haven, 1980).

[5]*See*, J. Q. Wilson, op. cit. *supra* note 3, pp. 31–37.

[6]Proof of this thesis can be found in the fact that West Virginia has the lowest crime rate in the United States. Notwithstanding that our per capita income is forty-ninth among American states, and our unemployment rate among the highest, we nonetheless have little serious crime in comparison to neighboring states. The reason for this happy phenomenon is probably that the majority of West Virginians live in communities where the poor are not segregated from the middle class. We have a few large housing projects in our major cities, and every city has a slum area, but the interaction among

147

could live without being tied to public transportation. Second, desegregation and the 1964 Civil Rights Act made it possible for middle-class blacks and other minorities to escape from the inner cities.

In 1945 virtually all black Americans lived in segregated areas, although not necessarily in the urban North. From the end of the Second World War until the end of the 1960s, millions of blacks migrated from the rural South to the ghettos of northern cities like Chicago. Yet in those days the ghettos were far more "middle class" than they are today; there was nowhere for black doctors, lawyers, school teachers, merchants or skilled workers to live outside of the city ghettos. For example, if we take that part of the South Side of Chicago that contains the now infamous Robert Taylor Homes housing project, we can see a microcosm of what happened across urban America. In 1970, 37 percent of the population of this section of the South Side was below the poverty line; in 1980, 51 percent of the population was below the poverty line. In 1970, the unemployment rate was 9.5 percent; in 1980, it was 24.2 percent. In 1970, 40 percent of the residents of the neighborhood lived in families with a female head; in 1980, the number had grown to 72 percent. In 1980, of the 54,000 residents, 33,000 were on welfare.[7]

What all this means is that if crime is correlated with lower class status, and community crime control is some function of

all social classes is much higher in West Virginia than in the urban states. For example, most upper-middle class West Virginians live inside our cities and towns. We have almost no suburban areas, because people are unwilling to commute long distances to work. It would not occur to me to live more than ten minutes from my office. In West Virginia the highest crime rates, as a percentage of the county populations, occur not in our cities, but in rural areas where lower socio-economic class persons live together in isolated pockets.

[7]In my estimation, the best comprehensive explanation of how our cities deteriorated and a large underclass emerged—notwithstanding all of government's efforts to expand opportunities and reduce discrimination—is Nicholas Lemann's landmark article in the June and July 1986 issues of *The Atlantic Monthly*, "The Origins of the Underclass." I am indebted to him for the statistics just cited as well as for much of what follows in this chapter.

enforcing middle-class standards, there is little chance of community action solving the crime problem in the worst-off sections of the inner cities. This is simply because in the abject slums no community consensus on appropriate conduct can emerge that the community can then enforce. Studies have consistently shown that participation in voluntary organizations is largely a middle-class phenomenon. Participants tend to be in the middle-income range, married with children, house owners and well educated. Furthermore, these people tend to live in neighborhoods characterized by a shared set of norms regarding public behavior. Collective crime-prevention programs, then, like Neighborhood Watch, are more prevalent in middle-class neighborhoods with racial and economic homogeneity.[8]

What all of this means is that we understand the extremes. In a town like Palm Beach, Florida, (which I described in the last chapter) it is easy to: (1) raise the taxes necessary to support a good public police force; (2) supplement that police force with private security; (3) develop precise standards of appropriate public behavior; (4) enforce those standards through both formal and informal coercion; and (5) exclude most strangers and carefully watch those strangers who can't be excluded. Taken together, then, all these factors lead to a negligible crime rate and a very safe environment.

On the other hand, in the housing projects of the inner cities: (1) a majority of residents are single female heads of household and their minor children; (2) there are virtually no middle-class residents with organizational skills; (3) a high percentage of residents are involved in crime themselves; and (4) honest residents are terrified by their violent neighbors. Thus, it is impossible to organize any sort of community crime control. Therefore, it is with residential areas between the two extremes of Palm

[8]*See*, D. P. Rosenbaum, "The Theory and Research Behind Neighborhood Watch: Is It a Sound Fear and Crime Reduction Strategy?" *Crime and Delinquency*, January 1987.

Beach on the one hand and an inner-city housing project on the other that we are concerned.

Recent experience among black residents of lower-income neighborhoods in Washington, Houston and St. Louis seems to indicate that when the crime problem becomes bad enough, most neighborhoods that are not abject slums have sufficient consensus on the big issues and enough organizational skills to begin volunteer patrols. Consequently, while as late as 1988 most sociologists would have predicted that all neighborhoods with large numbers of poor residents would be impossible to organize, there is less pessimism in that regard today.

Not all neighborhoods, of course, are predominantly residential. There are many urban districts where people must come and go at all hours and that have few permanent residents. One such neighborhood is the Longwood Avenue section of Boston, which is composed of the greatest medical complex in the world. Along Longwood Avenue can be found the Harvard Medical School, Boston Children's Hospital, Brigham and Woman's Hospital and the Beth Israel Hospital. There are shops and even hotels for those staying with hospital patients, but hardly any permanent residents live in this district. Nonetheless, nurses, doctors, hospital maintenance workers, family and friends of patients, and patients themselves constantly come and go. Community crime control in the sense of neighborhood volunteers can do nothing to reduce the crime threat in such a district because there is no neighborhood. People don't have enough at stake to invest time and effort organizing patrols. The only workable response in this type of situation is private security police employed by Harvard and the hospitals—a type of security that is now available within the buildings but not on the street.

I have collected most of the newspaper reports about neighborhood crime-fighting that appeared during 1988 and the first half of 1989. From these contemporary news accounts, I infer that the neighborhoods most prone to self-help contain a mixture of social classes and racial groups, but are on the border with distinctly poorer neighborhoods from which criminals intrude with persistent regularity. Here is a typical description from the 7 August 1988 *Philadelphia Inquirer*:

> In this guerrilla war on drugs, words
> are the weapons, thin streamers of emerald
> ribbon the artillery.
>   Battles are waged with bullhorns and
> smoking barbecues, kaffeeklatsches and
> Xeroxed photos of glum young men accused of
> "selling poison to our children and
> destroying our neighborhood."
>   So goes the bitter combat by press
> release and public protest that has spread
> this year like a little blitzkrieg from
> neighborhoods of narrow rowhouses in South
> Philadelphia to fading, elegant Victorian
> twins that tower over tree-shaded Germantown
> streets and one of the city's thriving drug
> bazaars.
>   "If you don't get out of our
> neighborhoods, some of us will deal with you
> personally," Frances Walker scolded a
> suspected drug dealer by name during a
> neighborhood anti-drug rally on North Farson
> Street in West Philadelphia last week.

Newsday, on Long Island, New York, ran this story datelined Houston, Texas, 19 September 1988:

> Kit van Cleave is loaded for bear—red
> beret, white T-shirt and as much attitude as
> a genteel, 48-year-old college professor can
> muster.
>   Sydney, poured into a sky-blue
> minidress, is a transvestite hooker with

skinny legs, looking for love and a quick
buck along Westheimer Boulevard.

In the thick soup of a steamy August
night in Texas, they square off in the
neighborhood of Montrose, a morose scrap of
forsaken urban landscape that borders
downtown and where burned-out nightclubs
and neglected two-story houses mix with the few
remaining well-maintained residences.

"Sorry, sir, but you'll have to leave,"
says van Cleave, arms folded, rocking gently
on her heels.

The hooker contorts his face into a mask
of disbelief. Command ignored, Sydney
lurches ahead uncertainly in a pair of white
pumps, courting potential suitors. Van
Cleave, however, strides behind him sucking
deliberately on a Marlboro, blanked by three
others in red caps.

"God, I wish these people would stop
following me," the hooker whines. Ten minutes
pass; crowds are bad for business, and
possible customers are chased. So, too, is
Sydney, who finally disappears in the
blackness of nearby Stanford Street.

One last representative piece comes from the 18 August 1988
edition of the Seattle *Times*:

It's the middle of the night, and 73-
year-old Warren Bronson climbs up the stairs
to the second story window overlooking his
neighborhood. He looks out and listens: no
shadowy figures, no unfamiliar noises. Good.

Call it night watch.

Bronson and his Alki-area neighbors
consider themselves an informal army. Their

marching orders are biblical: You *are* your
neighbor's keeper.

Tomorrow will mark the 15th year Seattle
residents like Bronson have watched over each
other as part of the Block Watch program, a
city-backed strategy to help people fight
crime in their neighborhoods.

The program has grown from 100 blocks in
1973 to 2,800 blocks this year. That
translates into a formidable force from
48,000 households from Broadview to Rainier
Beach—more than 20 percent of the homes in
the city, according to Mark Howard, director
of the Community Crime Prevention Department,
which oversees the program.

The program has given homeowners a
strong sense of security—and criminals a
lot of insecurity . . .

What comes through clearly in these three representative articles reporting on community self-help is that the neighborhoods
involved are racially and ethnically mixed, they contain a high
percentage of "solid citizens" with middle-class values, yet they
border areas with a high concentration of the underclass and have
become high-crime areas themselves because of intrusion by
outsiders. In the reports that I have quoted we see three typical
profiles of citizen action these days. Yet, of the three, the one
with the lowest likelihood of success is the first, from Philadelphia, where moral outrage has led more to political demonstrations and exhortations to improve public enforcement than to
concerted, long-term neighborhood action.

Both the police and the leaders of the neighborhood watch in
Seattle think highly of the Block Watch program and maintain
that it has significantly lowered the crime rate. A Seattle police
study indicates that in the Block Watch neighborhoods the crime
rate has been reduced between 48 and 61 percent. To achieve

such success, however, requires the type of sustained active "watching" that was described in the story. In most neighborhoods with "neighborhood watch" signs posted, researchers report that residents usually watch only passively; the result is no reduction in the crime rate. Furthermore, in most neighborhoods with watch programs, the active participation rate is very low, even when significant efforts are made by professional organizers to elicit community involvement.[9]

Finally, in the Houston story we have an example of the model that offers the highest likelihood of achieving long-term success. In the Houston example people are well enough organized to have distinctive uniforms; there is enough manpower (or womanpower) to back up one individual trying to make it hot for a misdemeanor-committing intruder; and, the group is well enough trained not to violate the criminal intruder's civil liberties, carry weapons or incite violence of any sort. Although the type of mass protest described in the Philadelphia story can focus the attention of the police on the problems of one neighborhood for a short time, and picketing drug dealers can move them momentarily on to other areas, only good organization and persistent efforts such as we see in Seattle (where efforts focus on nighttime property crime) and Houston (where efforts focus on ridding the neighborhood of low-level criminals who reduce the quality of life) can have any long-term effect.

In the neighborhoods that concern us most—those urban areas that are close to concentrations of the underclass—there are actually three separate but related problems that are grouped under the general heading "crime." The first does not actually involve crime at all, but rather the *threat* of crime and its corollary, *fear* of crime. Neighborhoods that are populated with diverse, disreputable persons appear to be unsafe to the average

[9]*See*, F. DuBow, M. McPherson and G. Silloway, "Organizing for the State: Neighborhood Watch as a Strategy of Community Crime Prevention," paper presented at the annual meeting of the American Society of Criminology, San Diego, 1985.

law-abiding citizen when those disreputable persons are easily recognized and prominent in public places. Thus, panhandlers, prostitutes, drunks, groups of loitering teenagers and drug dealers all make neighborhoods *feel* unsafe, notwithstanding that none of these individuals is necessarily a direct threat in terms of an immediate intent to commit a crime upon a stranger.[10] When a large, disheveled male approaches an obviously weaker person asking for money, there is always an implied threat, notwithstanding that the chap is but a panhandler. The person being panhandled has no idea whether the stranger approaching him has a concealed weapon, whether the stranger is crazy or whether some type of scene on the street might ensue.

Loitering teenagers present an even greater apparent menace. Studies have shown that many adult Americans of both sexes in the big cities will cross to the other side of the street upon the approach of just one teenager, and that a majority will cross to the other side of the street upon the approach of three or more. Both panhandlers and teenagers may be entirely benign in terms of their actual criminal intent, but they do not look benign to the average resident. This appearance of a crime threat prompts defensive measures such as staying inside, crossing to the other side of the street or avoiding any neighborhood with teenagers or panhandlers entirely. The reason that ordinary people react so

[10]Sometimes, the effects on a community of disreputable persons can be ironic. My literary agent lived for many years far uptown in New York City at 181st Street and Fort Washington Avenue. Her neighborhood was full of Dominican drug dealers who largely minded their own business, which, of course, was selling drugs. However, the presence of big-time drug dealers had the effect of keeping ordinary street crime at a minimum in that particular neighborhood. The standard hit-and-run criminals understood that the Dominicans would kill them without a second thought! Like other businessmen, the Dominicans were interested in the "business climate" and wanted good "community relations." Specifically, the Dominicans wanted to avoid drawing the police into their neighborhood for *any* reason. Consequently, although someone like my agent was always fearful of being caught up in a crossfire between rival drug gangs, she was not anxious about being mugged or raped; the drug dealers were perfectly friendly to the ordinary law-abiding residents who, in turn, tolerated them, *faute de mieux*, because the drug dealers protected the neighborhood.

defensively even though they appreciate that the apparent danger is far greater than the actual danger is that they believe that if they do become crime victims no one will be around to help them.

It is in this area of fear of crime that the studies demonstrate that New York's Guardian Angels have been most successful. Although there is little or no statistical correlation between Guardian Angel patrols and a reduction in mugging, purse snatching and rape in the subways, there is a very high correlation between Guardian Angel patrols and a greater appearance of safety. In a 1986 survey of New York City civilians, 75 percent approved the actions of the Guardian Angels, 61 percent wished that there were more Guardian Angels and 67 percent believed that the Guardian Angels make the subways safer.[11] Because *fear* of crime leads to expensive and inconvenient countermeasures (e.g., taxis instead of subways or buses, and staying in at night), it is no mean feat simply to reduce the appearance of danger and give ordinary people a sense of security.

Furthermore, those who commit only so-called victimless crime are really a much greater menace than they would at first appear. Drug dealers and prostitutes bring with them their customers, pimps, suppliers and rivals—all of whom create real or apparent danger. Studies such as the *Figgie Report on Fear of Crime* characterize the crime threat as "slowly paralyzing American society." The report found that fear of violence directly affects four of ten Americans and indirectly affects roughly 70 percent of the population. Many polls, such as a Gallup Poll conducted in March 1981, reveal that over one-half of the public is afraid to walk at night in the area surrounding their home.[12] Whenever a neighborhood has a visible population of pimps, prostitutes, drug dealers and the assorted weirdos whom these

---

[11]*See*, Dennis Jay Kennedy, *op. cit.*, *supra*, chapt. 2 note 1.
[12]*General Social Surveys—1972–1985*, National Opinion Research Center, University of Chicago, 1985.

vice purveyors attract, the neighborhood appears dangerous and therefore becomes a frightening place in which to live.

The second discrete problem is actual crime, either violent crime, such as rape or robbery, or property crime, such as burglary or auto theft. Yet in 1986, only 36 out of every 1000 persons living in central cities were victims of violent crime, and only 80 out of 1000 were victims of theft. If we further refine the analysis, we find that: (1) violent crime rates are highest against black males overall; (2) higher against blacks than whites or members of other minority groups; (3) higher against unemployed persons—whether male, female, white or black—than against employed persons in their respective groups; (4) higher against males than females; and (5) lowest against white females.[13] What all this means is that outside the inner city slums, we are all much safer from *actual* crime than we usually imagine.

A graphic example of this fact emerges from a detailed inquiry into public safety in the New York subways, a place that most New York residents and tourists find threatening. According to a New York *Times* study, only 2.6 percent of all felonies reported in New York City in 1984 occurred in the subway system. This low rate of actual crime is the primary reason that there is little or no correlation between Guardian Angel patrols and measurable reductions in the subway crime rate. Objectively, there was only one murder on the subways for every 142 million trips, and one robbery for every 213,000 trips. For those who avoided the most dangerous stations that had ramps, posts and connecting passageways (mostly in midtown Manhattan), the rates were much lower. In all of 1984 there were but twenty-one reported rapes in the New York subway system.[14] What that means, then, is that most of us *feel* that we are in much greater danger from

[13]U.S. Department of Justice, Office of Justice Programs, Bureau of Justice Statistics, *BJS Data Report*, 1988.

[14]J. Rangel, "Statistically, At Least, It Is Rather Safe Down There," *New York Times*, February 10, 1985.

crime than we really are, but that doesn't eliminate our fears and the defensive behavior that those fears induce.

Finally, the third discrete problem is vice—particularly drugs. Drugs are a problem for the law-abiding because drug addicts are likely to commit crimes to support their habits, and because drugs destroy the lives of our children and friends. The effects of drugs appear prominently under the first two problems we have discussed, namely disorder in the neighborhood and actual crime, but the sale and distribution of drugs present peculiar problems. The first, presented in Chapter 2, concerns the extraordinary level of violence that drug dealers are willing to employ to protect their business. The second is that much drug dealing goes on in private places where the general public and police officers without warrants have no right to be. Crack houses are nonetheless "houses" that have an owner and/or lessee whose rights to privacy are no less than anyone else's.

I have divided the crime problem into three separate, discrete components, primarily to help overcome possible objections to the proposition that well-organized and well-trained neighborhood patrols will significantly reduce crime. Liberal professors are fond of pointing out that dramatic increases in the number of police have never reduced the crime rate. For example, between 1954 and 1974 the size of the New York Police Department increased by 54 percent while the civilian population of the city remained nearly constant. Crime, however, increased faster than the police. This same phenomenon has been observed in different forms across the country where numbers of police have been dramatically increased over short periods, with little reduction in crime. This can be explained, however, primarily by what the police normally do—in other words, their reactive rather than active *modus operandi*.

Fortunately, there have also been experiments in which the police were not only increased, but also instructed to perform a more active patrolling function. These experiments have been sufficiently successful to overcome the negative findings associated with general increases in police-force manpower. Of these experiments, the most famous occurred in 1954 in New York City when the New York Police Department conducted a controlled study in East Harlem. Beginning on 1 September 1954, the police strength assigned to the Twenty-fifth Precinct in Manhattan was more than doubled. Most of the additional men were inexperienced recent graduates of the Police Academy who were assigned to walking patrols. These foot patrolmen were then supplemented with detectives, traffic cops, juvenile officers and members of the narcotics squad. The experiment was called Operation 25, and during its progress no foot post was left unmanned, although previously as many as two-thirds of the officially designated beats had been unmanned. Furthermore, during the experiment the number of foot patrol posts was increased from fifty-five to eighty-nine, and the area assigned each officer was significantly reduced to give greater in-depth focus to any single officer's observations.

During the four months that Operation 25 was in place, all serious crime declined, but the reduction was greatest for street crime that occurred in public places. Muggings fell from sixty-nine during the same period in 1953 to seven during the experiment; auto thefts dropped from seventy-eight to twenty-four; and burglaries, particularly where entry was made from the street into the front of the store or dwelling, declined as well. Crimes committed in private, however, remained unchanged. Thus there was no measurable decline in felonious assault—a crime frequently committed among friends or acquaintances—and the murder rate actually increased slightly from six to eight.[15]

Then, in 1960, the New York Police Department, in conjunction with the New York City Rand Institute, did another experiment along the same lines. In the Twentieth Precinct, po-

---

[15]See J. Q. Wilson, op.cit., supra, note 3, pp. 62–63.

lice manpower was increased by 40 percent, while in two similar neighboring precincts the manpower was left the same. The results were consistent with Operation 25: In the Twentieth Precinct, street robberies per week fell by 33 percent; auto theft per week fell by 49 percent; and grand larcenies "visible from the street" fell by 49 percent. Crimes committed in private places, however, like burglary, homicide and assault, appeared to show no reduction.[16]

Finally, in 1965 one of the most important experiments in policing ever done was conducted in the New York subway system. During the two years before 1965, crime had been increasing in the subways at about 50 percent a year. In April 1965, Mayor Robert Wagner ordered that the transit police force be increased from 1200 officers to just over 3100, with the object of providing one officer for every train and another for every station between the hours of 8:00 P.M. and 4:00 A.M.—the times of highest crime. Investigators analyzed the effect of this increase in manpower over an eight-year period, and the results have been used by just about everyone in the crime control business to prove just about every proposition anyone wants to prove.

In a nutshell, New York City found that immediately after the introduction of the additional transit police crime rates fell dramatically in the subways. But within a year or so, the number of subway robberies began to rise again rapidly. Indeed, by 1970 there were six times as many robberies as had occurred in 1965, before the addition of the new officers. However, these statistics—while perhaps standing for the proposition that crime is easily displaced from areas of intensive patrolling to less guarded areas—do not destroy the argument in favor of patrolling. Rather, it turns out, the number of subway felonies occurring per hour during the night fell in 1965 *and remained low*, while the number of felonies occurring during the day (after a brief decrease in

[16]*Ibid*, p. 64.

1965, immediately after the publicity concerning the new officers) increased steadily from 1965 on. Investigators from the New York City Rand Institute concluded that, although subway crime has tended to rise in general over the years, the addition of uniformed officers to the trains and stations *during the evening hours* has caused a significant reduction in crime during those hours.[17]

Other experiments have been conducted in places like Kansas City and rural South Carolina using expanded police manpower to patrol in cars. In both instances there were no measurable reductions in crime, which appears to indicate that the police presence must be intensely felt by would-be criminals in order for patrolling to be effective in preventing crime. This does not mean that in suburban neighborhoods nighttime patrols by volunteers in automobiles cannot reduce burglary, vandalism and auto theft. In the studies that show little correlation between patrolling and crime reduction, the police presence was very thin to begin with. Thus, even if such a police presence were doubled, there would not necessarily be a measurable increase in the surveillance *felt* by the criminal community. Therefore, comparisons of crime rates as police manpower increases or decreases tend to prove very little standing alone. The only important comparisons are between situations where there is such a thin police presence that would-be criminals have little fear of apprehension as the result of a patrol, and situations where there are sufficient police that would-be criminals are convinced of a high likelihood of apprehension by a patrol.

If the reader is asking himself or herself why the police departments haven't understood the result of the experiments I have described and inaugurated extensive foot patrols, one footnote to the New York subway story is in order. Studies have shown that in 1965 when the additional manpower was placed on the

[17]*Ibid*, p. 65.

trains and in the stations, it cost the City of New York roughly $35,000 for every felony that was deterred.[18] And $35,000 was worth about $130,000 in constant 1990 dollars. The reason that most New Yorkers supported the project, however, had less to do with deterring actual crime in the subways (the amount of which in absolute terms is fairly low even today) than it had to do with reducing the *fear* of crime. If we asked the cost in dollars per anxious moment avoided by an elderly passenger, single woman or well-dressed man because an officer was close by, then the cost becomes much more reasonable. Yet, as I indicated in the last chapter, the cost is far beyond most state and local governments' capacity to pay, given the current climate favoring fiscal conservatism and the political fights that inevitably arise over how public money should be spent. And that's why we have to do the job ourselves.

What types of organizations will allow us to do the job ourselves? To answer this question we must examine the resources available in a typical mixed community. Initially, as I pointed out in Chapter 3, most young and middle-aged adults are very busy. A majority of young families today require two incomes to live, so both partners work when work is available. Teenagers and college-age adults have time (and, as the Guardian Angels amply demonstrate, can be a major source of competent, enthusiastic manpower), and retired persons have time. For most mature adults, however, volunteer crime control will be perceived as a burden. Some community members will accept the responsibility, but most will probably "free ride" on the efforts of others. For some, however, restoring law and order may provide the same positive, creative opportunities that being active in a volunteer fire department provides.

Retired persons are good for organizing, fund raising, manning radios and telephones and watching neighborhoods from sta-

[18]*Ibid*, p. 66.

tionary positions (as in the Seattle story quoted earlier in the chapter.) Middle-aged adults—particularly middle-aged men—are the ideal personnel for leading patrols, but teenagers and young adults can also perform this function well. Yet for community crime control to work, many essential resources will probably need to come from the regular police. Studies have shown that few community crime-control efforts have been successful without the enthusiastic instigation and cooperation of the regular police. The one major exception to this rule is New York's Guardian Angels, who were intensely disliked by the official police and City Hall bureaucracy for many years. Although today relations appear to be improving between the Angels and the government, the police still seem to look upon the Guardian Angels with suspicion.

The main reason that relations between community patrols and the police are so important is that local government has money. Although community crime control is much cheaper than public policing, community crime control nonetheless costs more money than most blue-collar communities can come up with. In many areas, particularly suburbs where foot patrols are not practical, a good communications network is indispensable. Two-way radios, however, are expensive, as are portable video cameras, powerful searchlights and perhaps even night vision enhancing devices (called in the army "sniper scopes") that help identify illegal activity in dark areas. Although it will usually be possible to enlist a retired person to serve for free as "executive director," it will nonetheless be necessary to provide essential office equipment, stationery, postage and telephone service.

In addition, neighborhood patrolling is work not ideally done by complete amateurs. If we examine for a moment rural volunteer fire departments, it becomes obvious that volunteer firemen receive almost as much training as professionals. Fighting fires is difficult, highly dangerous work, and a person who does not understand how to approach gas mains safely or how to evaluate the likelihood of structural collapse at different stages of a fire, will get himself and his workmates killed. The same applies to community patrolling. The United States has an elaborate legal system that forbids certain conduct and protects other conduct. Thus there are both criminal laws and civil rights laws. It is important to know at least the rough outline of each, and it is even more important to know the points at which these laws collide. For example, while a citizen can arrest a person thought to have committed a felony at any time in a public place, even if the person making the arrest has not observed the crime, a citizen can arrest a person for a misdemeanor without a warrant *only* if the crime is being committed in the arresting person's presence.

Most volunteers, however, don't know the distinctions between felonies and misdemeanors and the law that governs each. At what point, for example, does theft change from petty larceny (a misdemeanor) to grand larceny (a felony)? The answer depends on the particular law of the state in which the crime occurs. In West Virginia, for example, what would be called a mugging in New York, which is considered a low-level crime there, is either aggravated robbery, which will land a perpetrator in the state prison for ten years to life, or unaggravated robbery, which will put him in prison for five to eighteen years.

Consequently, volunteer police, just like volunteer firemen, need extensive training, and the best place to obtain that training is from the official law enforcement establishment. State and local government regularly give cash grants to volunteer organizations to do useful things; in volunteer organizations labor costs are minimal and there is a high public return to the public money so invested. At another level, however, grants go with great regularity to organizations that have election-day political power. Fortunately, when it comes to a broad-based, community crime-control group, election-day political power should follow naturally if the group can sustain enthusiastic participation and a sense of moral outrage.

Although the relationship between the New York police and the Guardian Angels has not been a happy one, this relationship is the exception. In Seattle, the neighborhood crime watch is actually sponsored by the police, and that has been the general rule with most citizen groups. The key, perhaps, to good relations between volunteers and regular police is an early request for help in training and thorough coordination between police and volunteers. Of course, the biggest incentive to set up a neighborhood patrol is anger and frustration about the ineffectiveness of the regular police. But the wrong way to start a neighborhood group is with an "I'll show you" attitude toward the regular officers. One of the things that I hope the reader has come to appreciate from this book is that the regular police everywhere are overworked and underpaid.

In setting up a community crime-control group, effective lobbying is just as important as effective patrol leadership, good communications and good training. If the local police and political authorities favor a neighborhood crime-control group they can lend or give the group some very expensive resources, one of which is trained lawyers. Burning down a crack house, while perhaps satisfying, is not nearly as effective as seeking an injunction to tear the building down as a public nuisance. Any citizen can file such a petition, but only trained lawyers know how to prepare the papers. Lobbying, of course, requires being active in politics, and the basic rule there is that one must reward friends and punish enemies. A neighborhood group that can get two hundred voters to the polls who will all vote the "crime control" slate has instant credibility and something with which to bargain.

Another aspect of lobbying is public relations. Inevitably, opponents of neighborhood policing will levy charges of racism, elitism and Ku Klux Klanism. These charges should be anticipated in advance and efforts should be made to get interracial and interclass support. Traditionally, this is achieved by establishing a broad-based advisory board with representatives from all the constituencies that might be affected. Such a board would be too much trouble in a small, homogeneous neighborhood, but well worthwhile if the crime-control group is ambitious enough to want to take in a big territory composed of different neighborhoods.

From newspaper accounts of crime-control groups in 1988, 1989 and 1990, it appears that the drug crisis has motivated citizens to undertake action that is substantially more dangerous than the Seattle Block Watch described earlier or even the traditional suburban car patrol. When citizens become so furious that they are willing to undertake high-risk patrolling—as in the Houston example given earlier—then it is wise to think about life and disability insurance for members of the group who might be killed or injured. Although good training should keep these risks to a minimum, the general availability of handguns throughout America, combined with a savage underclass and a large number of lunatics, makes an accidental shooting a risk that should be contemplated and accommodated in advance. In some places—particularly with the help of state and local government—citizen crime-control groups may be able to qualify for workers' compensation coverage at reasonable rates, particularly if the group is incorporated. Patrolling is still much safer than most factory work, and it is much safer than mining, working on the railroads or trimming trees.

When we are talking about a group like the Guardian Angels, which is composed primarily of impecunious young persons, individual insurance against tort suits is not a compelling consideration. If a twenty-two-year-old from a blue-collar family is sued, the state exemptions from levy by a creditor will protect his few assets, and the federal bankruptcy code will allow him to declare bankruptcy and discharge any judgment that might be rendered against him in court. Furthermore, there are public legal services offices that will file bankruptcy petitions for free and legal clinics that will file them cheaply. More to the point, however, abjectly poor persons are seldom sued.

If we look at the homeowners of Seattle or the established middle-class families of Philadelphia, however, it becomes obvious (at least to lawyers) that active patrolling may, indeed, create dangerous civil liabilities. Suits for false arrest, assault, false imprisonment, civil rights violations and related causes of action are, at the very least, expensive to defend. Furthermore, notwithstanding efforts at training and weeding out of aggressive volunteers with authoritarian personalities, there will nonetheless be occasions when volunteer community police do bad things. Most of the time when that happens the victim will not sue because suits against any type of police are difficult to win and lawyers are reluctant to take such cases on contingent fees. Nonetheless, suits will be brought occasionally, and when victims do sue, it is possible for jury verdicts to be returned that can bankrupt the people involved and wipe out their life's savings.

Furthermore, under agency principles, if one member of an organization does everything right and is as solicitous of civil rights as Earl Warren would be, that does not necessarily protect him from liability for the tortious acts of other volunteers with whom he is associated in a common enterprise. Thus, if John is the watch commander one night and Charles, who is out on patrol, beats up a suspect, it is quite possible that John will be liable. Certainly, if John has more money than Charles, John will be dragged into the lawsuit and required to spend thousands of dollars in legal fees unless an insurance company stands behind the community patrol organization. Chapter 6 discusses this problem in more detail and explains how to incorporate a citizen crime-control group to reduce these problems.

This problem of liability should demonstrate just how important it is to exclude from crime-control organizations anyone who is aggressive, authoritarian or mentally unstable. Psychologists have developed tests for these traits that are regularly used by police departments and private guard companies, but formal testing is unlikely to be acceptable in a volunteer organization. Furthermore, the tests are hardly foolproof. Therefore, groups must closely monitor new members for the first six months and immediately expel members who violate the standard operating procedures. The Guardian Angels even go so far as to search each member about to leave on patrol to determine whether there are any unauthorized weapons. Constant reiteration of what members should *not* do, as well as a low group tolerance for unprofessional conduct, should be enough to drive the aggressive, authoritarian and unbalanced personality types out of the organization.

Much as we would like it to be otherwise, serious community patrolling inevitably involves a willingness to use force, and there is no way around that. When a woman yells "Rape!" she needs immediate intervention, and not a videotape of the rapist. Unarmed citizens are no match for heavily armed thugs, but the average rapist, housebreaker, drug dealer or car thief is not armed, nor are the roving bands of juvenile rowdies who so often make neighborhoods unlivable. Except in a few states that have narrowed the common-law power of citizen's arrest by statute, citizens are allowed to use reasonable, nondeadly force to apprehend and arrest law breakers. But, as with the official police, resort to force will inevitably lead to some abuses; therefore, volunteers who undertake to apprehend suspects should carry liability insurance.

Insurance not only protects the volunteers, it also has two other valuable effects: Insurance guarantees that victims of overzealous patrolling will receive compensation, and insurance guarantees good supervision, good training, and good standard operating procedures, because the insurer is even more interested than the volunteers in seeing that everything be done exactly right. Insurance, however, is a complicated matter. Michael Prins, executive vice president of Frank B. Hall & Co. of Minnesota, one of America's largest commercial insurance brokers, told me that it would be impossible to place liability insurance for a volunteer police force today. The liability is open-ended, and companies have no actuarial experience by which they can estimate their potential exposure and calculate premiums.

Mr. Prins assured me, however, that if a state passes a statute giving volunteer police the same immunities and damage limits regular police enjoy, Frank B. Hall & Co. Inc. could find an affordable policy with a little arm twisting. (A model statute meeting these requirements can be found in Appendix A to Chapter 6.) An "affordable policy" turns out to cost between one hundred and two hundred dollars per year per volunteer, depending on the state's damage caps and its courts' track record in tort litigation. The insurer, of course, would cover the cost of any lawsuit brought against a volunteer.

I asked Mr. Prins how he placed insurance for private security guards. He said that insurance for private guards is also difficult to place, but insurers can at least predict their exposure with sufficient precision to set premiums. Private guards have been around for a long time, risk information is available and guards are employed by businesses that are motivated by economic rather than political considerations. Businesses have incentives to avoid litigation, so guards are screened for psychotic personalities and are constantly admonished not to be overzealous. Yearly liability coverage typically costs two hundred dollars per guard.

If, however, each individual involved in a volunteer police group must ante up two hundred dollars each year as a condition of membership, it will be difficult to recruit volunteers. Here again we encounter the need for official support. In many locales, the government has boards of risk management that purchase insurance for government employees, or manage a system that combines self-insurance with some type of private reinsurance for large exposures. The ideal solution to the insurance problem is to put a local crime-control group under this public umbrella, but the likelihood of accomplishing that is small given the fiscal demands made on government at all levels. Alternatively, businesses within a community protected by volunteers may be willing to underwrite some of the insurance costs, particularly if there is a measurable decline in rowdy behavior, property crimes and violence. But soliciting money must be done with great circumspection; without careful management, volunteers may begin to look like extortionists running the classic protection racket. Indeed, some criticism has been levied against the Guardian Angels in this regard.

I have been a lawyer all my adult life, but I have also been a businessman and a politician. The businessman in me constantly reminds the lawyer in me that lawyers are the world's greatest deal killers. The job of lawyers is to be careful and to insulate their clients from all possible risk, either known or unknown. Although things like death, disability and general liability insurance are "lawyerly" considerations that should be taken into account in an ideal world, dwelling on them at too great length is likely to discourage any type of neighborhood policing.

But exactly because death and disability are real possibilities, and exactly because serious litigation is also a real possibility, the second best approach—in the absence of insurance—is to arrange standard operating procedures that minimize these problems. The police have such standard operating procedures, and they are probably as good a model as any to copy. As Mr. Prins at Frank B. Hall & Co. has pointed out, the experience with private guards has been largely positive. But that is because the for-profit companies that hire private guards are interested in the bottom line and not in vindicating their sense of righteous indignation. Private companies want the policing job done at minimum cost, including litigation costs.

To summarize the host of considerations upon which this chapter has touched, we can say that the elements that work include: (1) uniforms that capitalize on easy recognition by both would-be perpetrators and ordinary citizens; (2) avoidance of all situations likely to escalate into serious violence, particularly violence involving firearms; (3) good communication by radios and telephones to the official police to handle dangerous situations; (4) reliance upon equipment like searchlights, video cameras, night vision enhancers, and careful note-taking to identify perpetrators, preserve evidence, and provide witnesses; (5) avoidance of dangerous confrontations with perpetrators who may be armed and savage; (6) intensive training using the official police to develop standard operating procedures that minimize both the risk to volunteers and the likelihood that civilians will be abused or have their civil rights violated; (7) political organization to elicit funds from local authorities to help defray equipment and out-of-pocket operating costs; and, (8) death, disability and liability insurance.

Because insurance, while an ideal solution to many problems, is unlikely to be available or affordable to the average community volunteer police group, cop nuts and other psychologically unstable personalities cannot be allowed to join. And the enthusiasm of young males who believe themselves to be immortal and are searching for opportunities to prove their virility must be tempered by leadership from retired policemen and older males who served under combat conditions in the armed forces. Volunteer community police organizations have no place for youngsters so immature that they cannot appreciate the dangers inherent in confrontations with unknown criminals and the danger to the life's savings of older members from lawsuits. And at the head of the list of what doesn't work is any type of firearm. In addition, defensive weapons like billy clubs and Mace should be used sparingly, and when used at all should serve a symbolic rather than literal function.

There is no one ideal model that will work everywhere. Urban neighborhoods require different techniques from the suburbs; neighborhoods next door to slums require more intensive patrolling than neighborhoods farther removed from the slums; big city housing projects probably have so many problems that nothing but relocating the law-abiding to other environs will work; and rural areas have such a large territory in comparison to the population that no feasible amount of increased patrolling is likely to reduce crime. But, regardless of the specific patrolling or surveillance techniques selected for *any* community, if the considerations discussed in this chapter are kept firmly in mind there is a high probability of reducing crime, with no loss to civil rights and civil liberties.

Chapter VI

PRACTICAL CONSIDERATIONS AND FORMS

Table of Contents for Forms and Checklists

There is no substitute for the advice of a local lawyer when setting up a civic organization. Although many legal rules are shared among states, each state still has at least some peculiar and/or eccentric requirements that only a local practitioner understands. Therefore, broad generalizations about American law are not just unhelpful; they can actually be dangerously misleading. Nonetheless, with that introductory warning, I shall now discuss in a general way laws governing community crime-control groups. My intention, however, is not to give specific legal advice, but rather to give the reader only a general feel for the most urgent legal problems that are likely to arise and to suggest ways to avoid at least some of them.

In this chapter I discuss a crime-control group's legal liabilities and explain how incorporation can reduce individual members' risks. I also discuss the rules governing citizen's arrest and propose two statutes which, if passed by state legislatures, will reduce liability exposure and make groups more insurable. In a similar vein, I have included some model standard operating procedures which, if followed, should reduce the number of complaints, bad editorials and lawsuits. There is a model corporate charter with accompanying model corporate bylaws for setting up a nonprofit corporation, and I give a step-by-step guide to applying for federal tax-exempt status. The table of contents above directs the reader to these specific forms and checklists. The rest of the chapter is a commentary on why these procedures are useful and how to use the forms.

i. Lawsuit Economics

My law clerk once worked on a case in Alabama in which a family wanted to sue for the tragic death of a two-year-old child. The child's grandfather was driving his Volkswagen van in the suburbs of Mobile, with the little girl standing on the passenger's seat. As the van approached a convenience store, some lout of a driver in a souped-up, sporty sedan, pulled right out in front of the van, oblivious to the traffic. The grandfather yanked the wheel of the van, veering into another lane and away from the lout's car. This motion pitched the little girl out of the open window next to which she was standing. The child hit the pavement and was then struck by the back wheels of the van, killing her instantly.

Who was to blame? The driver who was oblivious to what traffic was coming? The grandfather who might have veered the other way or not allowed the car window to be open with a child standing on the seat? The child's mother, who should have insisted on an approved child seat with appropriate restraint devices? No doubt all these people played some part in the little girl's death. Most people, if required to place the blame on one person, would probably blame the driver of the souped-up sedan. But whom would you sue?

If you said "the lout driver," you'd flunk out of law school. Why? Needless to say, a driver this bad is uninsured or carries the bare, statutory minimum insurance that allows him to register his car. He's a bad man, but he's not worth a nickel and not worth your time for a moral victory. Ditto for the child's own mother or grandfather, who, in any event, are part of the family bringing the suit.

Actually, the deep-pocket defendant who ended up being sued and getting stuck with a $150,000 judgment to the little girl's family was the R. J. Reynolds Tobacco Company! This is because there was a sign just off the roadside next to the convenience store, advertising Winston cigarettes. The plaintiff's lawyer's theory of liability was that the lout driver must have had his view blocked by the sign. Thus the plaintiffs sued Reynolds, who provided the sign, and the owners of the store, who put the sign up. The driver was not sued, but he did testify as he was instructed by the plaintiffs, who bought his testimony with an agreement not to sue him. The plaintiffs requested a jury trial, and the jury's award of $150,000 was a compromise, down from the $5 million figure initially thrown out in deliberations, because *one* juror maintained that the R. J. Reynolds company and the convenience-store owners hadn't done anything wrong.

The moral of the story, as every plaintiff's lawyer learns who has sued a poor person and then tried to collect, is that there's no sense suing until you sniff out some money to collect when you win. The corollary, naturally, is that poor people can do whatever the hell they want to do to other people, short of serious crime, because no one will ever bother to sue them. If someone does sue, he collects a moral victory, that is, one that won't pay his lawyer's fee. Obviously, lawyers who work for "contingent fees" (i.e., fees that are paid only if there is a recovery) are reluctant to take such cases.

These are important considerations for community crime-control groups. Anyone who tries to enforce the law makes himself a lightning rod for civil lawsuits. Indeed, as chief justice of a state supreme court, I am sued at least once a year because of some action that I have taken as a judge. So far no one has recovered a judgement, but if I were not insured by the State of West Virginia and did not have lawyers available to defend me at no personal expense, I would be reluctant to continue to serve as a judge. In a similar vein, although defending a civil lawsuit takes a regular policeman away from his street duties, he isn't worried about the money. His department pays the damages for him. The same is true for private security guards working for insured corporations.

Citizen patrol groups are different. They are unlikely to have a rich group behind them to pay for their mistakes unless they are well enough organized and well enough financed to buy insurance. Therefore, if money must be paid, it must come from the group itself or from the members of the group personally. A large judgment can easily bankrupt a group or its members. Yet, if the members of the group are relatively poor, the hazard is minimal. State and federal law provide that several thousand dollars of equity in a home are exempt from creditors even when a person declares federal bankruptcy, and there are additional exemptions (such as farm implements and the tools of the trade)[1] that guarantee that the typical member of, say, the Guardian Angels, has little to fear from a lawsuit. When wages are garnished, a debtor with nothing of value but his wages can file for personal bankruptcy in federal court and discharge a debt forever with no costs other than the filing of the bankruptcy petition. If a person has property in excess of the applicable state and federal exemptions, however, he or she can lose everything in a lawsuit, to say nothing of the legal fees incurred in defense. Therefore, anyone who shows a positive net worth on a balance sheet beyond a few thousand dollars of home equity should be concerned with personal liability when he or she joins a crime-control group.

II. NONPROFIT CORPORATIONS

Because citizen crime-control groups may attract civil lawsuits for large sums of money, the way the group organizes itself makes a big difference. There are basically two options: an unincorporated association or a nonprofit corporation. As a general rule, the richer the members of the group, the more important it becomes to be organized in *corporate* form and to have a good policy of liability insurance.

An unincorporated association is not a distinct legal entity. It simply consists of its members. Unless formal steps are taken to create a corporation, any civic organization is an unincorporated association. The major advantages of forming an unincorporated association are that it is cheap and easy. The major disadvantage, however, of remaining unincorporated is personal liability—that is, the officers might have to pay for the debts and wrongdoing of the association. In an unincorporated association, unlike a corporation, there is no separate legal entity for strangers to sue,

[1] *See* 11 U.S.C.§ 522 [1986].

so strangers must sue individual members. This can be devastating—just ask anyone who has ever been sued. Although the chances of being sued may be slim, because lawyers know that unless there has been outrageous conduct most jurors will side with the vigilantes, all lawsuits are risks that most of us would rather not face.

How many people drive without car insurance? Quite a few, actually, but they generally do it because they can't afford to pay the insurance premiums. And if they can't afford to pay for insurance, chances are they haven't got anything to lose if they *are* sued. This is why most states now require basic insurance as a condition of registering a motor vehicle, but even where statutes require coverage, the limits are so low as to be useless to a victim who is seriously injured.

People who have nothing to lose in a lawsuit are relatively free in their behavior. As long as they don't do anything that is criminal, their behavior is immune from attack. In lawyers' talk, a poor person is said to be "judgment proof." Because he has no assets, no one will bother to sue him. If someone did sue, he would find the experience most unfulfilling and one-sided. The poor defendant would probably lose the case by default— a hollow victory for the plaintiff who still wouldn't collect a dime.

Thus it is all well and good for very poor people to form a citizen protection group on a shoestring, with a minimum of organization. This has happened in many of the poorest neighborhoods of American cities. Neighbors just get fed up and take to the streets with signs, vocally taunt the drug dealers, organize community patrols against muggers, car thieves and vandals, and attempt to destroy the markets for drugs and crack houses.

The problems come in the neighborhoods where the people aren't poor enough to act with impunity. People don't have to be rich by any standard to worry about being sued. Anyone who owns a house with more equity than the typical $5000 state-bankruptcy exemption, or has a decent job and a good credit rating has something to worry about. It should be remembered that a person can declare federal bankruptcy only once every six years.[2] Thus, one baseball bat and one cracked head could equal one house lost to an injured street thug, years of garnished wages or bankruptcy. And the one who loses his house doesn't have to be the one who cracked the thug's head. If you are an officer of an unincorporated association, and an association member on patrol cracks an innocent person's head, you, as an officer, can be sued as well.

It is this cracked head problem that incorporation may solve. Corporations were originally formed precisely to shield investors from personal liability for business debts. At the dawn of the industrial revolution, the refinement of incorporation principles facilitated the efficient pooling of capital by reducing each participating investor's personal risks. Debts of a corporation must normally be collected only from the assets of the corporation, not from the corporation's shareholders or officers. People who deal with a corporation normally understand this, and it is considered fair to corporate creditors to restrict their debt-collection to the corporation itself.[3] The same idea has been extended to nonprofit corporations because it is in the public interest for charities to incorporate; people will be more likely to enter charitable undertakings if they do not open themselves up to unlimited personal liability by doing so.

[2]Generally, 11 U.S.C.§ 727 [1986] bars a discharge in a liquidation or Chapter 7 case if the debtor has been granted a discharge ''within six years before the date of the filing of the [bankruptcy] petition.''

[3]A corporation's creditors can be divided into two groups: voluntary creditors and involuntary creditors. Voluntary creditors are those who agree to do business with the corporation and can either accept or reject the corporation as a worthy credit risk. Voluntary creditors, like banks, will often not accept just the liability of the corporation and will demand, in addition, a ''personal guarantee'' by some solvent individual. Involuntary creditors, on the other hand, are persons who are owed money by the corporation because of some action taken by the corporation, such as causing an injury or interfering with a business transaction, that was beyond the control of the creditor.

Courts are often uncomfortable with the insulation from personal liability that corporate status provides. Therefore, when courts find fraud or other wrongdoing on the part of corporate officers or employees, the courts will often "pierce the corporate veil" and hold individuals associated with a corporation personally liable to a corporation's creditors. This is particularly the case with respect to involuntary creditors like those injured by the negligence of the corporation's employees. Decisions concerning whether to pierce the corporate veil are context specific, so that general rules give little practical guidance. Therefore, it is important for nonprofit corporations dedicated to crime control to cultivate the good will of the courts by working hard to do everything right so that there is no systemic, outrageous conduct that would lead a judge to *want* to pierce the corporate veil.

The theory of incorporation requires that each corporation be treated as a separate entity, as if it were a person. This gives the corporation the benefit of longevity. A corporation's owners, officers and employees come and go, but the corporation continues to exist regardless of changes in personnel. For organizations like neighborhood crime-control groups this can be important because many such groups today are founded and sustained by the vision of one leader, for example Curtis Sliwa of the Guardian Angels, and the loss of that leader can be devastating to an informal organization. Corporate identity provides a smooth mechanism for passing leadership on to new generations of volunteers, and because a corporation has a charter and by-laws, there is an orderly way to elect leaders and settle internal disputes.

A corporation is a "person" in the eyes of the law; therefore, a corporation has the right to own property in its own name, make contracts with employees and merchants and sue in the courts. The right to own property is significant for any civic organization that hopes to establish an endowment for its future use. The right to form contracts makes it easier to rent office space. The right to sue in the courts makes it easier for a crime-control group to go into court to have a crack house condemned as a nuisance or a firetrap.

The use of the nonprofit corporation form to organize a group also gives the group more respectability with donors. Donors may be reluctant to give money to an unincorporated association because of uncertainty about whether the group will be around the next year to spend the money as the donor wishes and because usually there is no tax deduction. In an unincorporated association, it is all too easy for the group to disband over some dispute and for the group's leaders to abscond with money meant to carry out the charitable purposes. The corporate form offers stability. Donors can be more sure of how their money is being used, and the other members of the group can, too. Corporate organization gives a clear sense of the group's policies and plans for the future, as well as the chain of command within the group.

For purposes of liability, a nonprofit corporation has a much better chance of finding insurance than does a loosely organized association. An insurance company wants to insure only known risks, those that can be mathematically calculated from past experience. A corporation, as a stable entity, can build up a track record in a neighborhood, which it can then present to an insurance company in the hope of obtaining a liability policy. Where the dimensions of the risk to be assumed are hard for the insurance company to calculate, the company may not offer to insure the group at all, or charge premiums so high that the group can't afford a policy. Insurance companies routinely insure private guards at reasonable rates, so it becomes possible to convince insurance companies that the risks in a neighborhood crime-control group are roughly those that they have already calculated with regard to private guards.

To form a corporation, the organizers must draw up a corporate charter (also called "articles of incorporation"), which will serve as a kind of constitution for the corporation. The proposed corporate charter is then filed along with an application for corporate status and a fee with the state government. To govern the day-to-day activities of the group, the corporation elects a board of directors and draws up a set of bylaws. The forms in Appendix B provide sample articles of incorporation and sample bylaws that meet the applicable legal requirements in most states.

III. TAX-EXEMPT STATUS

An important consideration for any civic group is fund-raising. It is also important that the group get the maximum possible usage of any funds it raises. It is thus essential that any civic group qualify for exemption from federal income taxes. There are two kinds of exemptions. The first allows the nonprofit group to avoid paying taxes on the money the group raises or generates in its operations. To qualify, a group need only demonstrate that it is a nonprofit group (that is, not a business corporation) and that it is organized for some civic or charitable purpose. The second kind of tax exemption allows people who donate to the group to write off their donations as deductions from their own income for federal and state tax purposes. This is obviously a bonus in fund-raising because it means that in most states about 34 percent of any contributions made is paid by the federal and state governments through tax deductions.

In order for an incorporated neighborhood crime-control group to be exempt from federal income taxes under section 501(a) of the federal *Internal Revenue Code,* the corporation must meet the descriptions for organizations found in section 501(c) of the Code.[4] To establish tax-exempt status the corporation must com-

[4]Certain other organizations may qualify for an exemption under the Code. Examples include religious and apostolic associations [section 501(d)], cooperative hospital service organizations [section 501(e)], cooperative service organizations of operating educational organizations (section 501(f)), farmers' cooperative associations (section 521) or pension, profit-sharing and stock bonus plans (section 401(a)).

plete a determination letter request on Internal Revenue Service (IRS) Form 1023 or Form 1024 within fifteen months after the end of the month in which the corporation was created. Internal Revenue Service Form 1023 is used to apply for a ruling on the corporation's exempt status under section 501(c)(3) of the Code. Form 1023 also fulfills the notice requirements of sections 508(a) and (b) of the Code. A user fee must be submitted with a determination letter request.

The fee is computed by completing IRS Form 8718, User Fee for Exempt Organization Determination Letter Request, that should be filed with a determination letter request. After receiving a determination letter request and fee, the IRS will issue either a favorable or an adverse determination letter. An adverse determination can be appealed. With any adverse determination letter, the IRS should include their publication *Exempt Organization Appeal Procedures*, Publication 892, which contains information necessary for an appeal. The tax-exempt organization must also file annual information with the IRS even if the application for exempt status is pending or in the appeal process. Form 990, Return of Organization Exempt from Income Tax, fulfills the annual filing requirement.

A community crime-control group should be considered a charitable organization and thus exempt under section 501(c)(3) of the *Internal Revenue Code*. The current treasury regulations state that the term "charity" is used "in its generally accepted legal sense . . . [and] the broad outlines . . . as developed by judicial decisions."[5] Donors may deduct contributions to the crime-

---

[5]Treas. Reg. § 1.501(c)(3)–1(d)(2) [1989] provides the following examples:

[Charity] includes: Relief of the poor and distressed or of the underprivileged; advancement of religion; advancement of education or science; erection or maintenance of public buildings, monuments, or works; lessening of the burdens of Government; and promotion of social welfare by organizations designed to accomplish any of the above purposes, or (i) to lessen neighborhood tensions; (ii) to eliminate prejudice and discrimination; (iii) to defend human and civil rights secured by law; or (iv) to combat community deterioration and juvenile delinquency.

prevention corporation recognized as exempt under section 501(c)(3) of the Code.

A community crime-control group that incorporates also meets the definition of a social welfare organization, an exempt organization under section 501(c)(4).[6] The major distinction between an organization whose exemption is recognized under section 501(c)(4) rather than 501(c)(3) is that contributions to a 501(c)(4) organization are *not* deductible by donors. If a corporation plans to attempt to influence legislation by active campaigning, the corporation cannot be exempted under section 501(c)(3)—in other words, contributions are not tax free—and must apply under section 501(c)(4).[7] However, *contributions to 501(c)(4) organizations can qualify as business expenses for donors who can show a reasonable relationship between legitimate business needs and the lobbying carried out by the crime control group.* Thus, although ordinary householders would not be able to deduct contributions from their taxes, a local convenience store, shopping mall or warehouse that could show that the crime control group was pursuing political action that would lower the incidence of crime costly to its business could deduct the contribution as a business expense. In this instance, the amount of the business expense is not restricted.

Internal Revenue Service Form 1024 should be used to apply for a ruling on the corporation's tax-exempt status under section 501(c)(4) of the Code. Form 1024 also fulfills any additional notice requirements.

[6]Treas. Reg.§ 1.501(c)(4)–1(a)(2)(i) [1989] states in pertinent part:

An organization is operated exclusively for the promotion of social welfare if it is primarily engaged in the promoting in some way the common good and general welfare of the people of the community.

[7]Campaigning by a 501(c)(4) organization is limited by Treas. Reg.§ 1.501 (c)(4)–1(a)(2)(ii) [1989] that states:

The promotion of social welfare does not include direct or indirect participation or intervention in political campaigns on behalf of or in opposition to *any candidate* for public office. (Emphasis added)

Forms 1023 and 1024 contain information and specific instructions about what is required to apply for exempt status. A crime-control organization must submit evidence to show that members are actively engaged in crime prevention and control, and the IRS should be informed whether the organization owns any equipment and whether the organization provides any specific benefits to members. The evidence submitted should show how the organization's crime-prevention and control activities will lessen the burden of government. Such evidence might include statements from: (1) law enforcement agencies—local, state or federal; (2) governmental units—city mayors, county commissioners, state legislators, prosecuting attorneys or the state attorney general; (3) persons or agencies who assist in setting up crime-control groups; or (4) other community-based organizations.

Forms 1023 and 1024 require that the organization have an employer identification number even if the organization does not have any employees. An Application for Employer Identification Number, Form SS-4, can be submitted with the application for exemption. If the organization does employ someone, immediate application should be made for an employer identification number. *Note: Employers, unless exempted, are responsible for withholding, depositing, paying and reporting federal income tax, social security taxes (FICA) and state workers' compensation and unemployment compensation premiums.* There may be additional withholding, depositing, paying and reporting requirements imposed on employers by state and local governments. I have made no attempt to specify these requirements because they vary so widely among the fifty states. A summary of employer responsibilities can be found in the IRS publication, Circular E, Publication 15, *Employer's Tax Guide.*

Tax-Exempt Status Check List and Publications

In order to apply for exempt status the organization should submit the following forms:

(1) Form 1023 pkg.   Application for Recognition for Exemption under Section 501(c)(3) of the Internal Revenue Code (form and instructions); or

Form 1024 pkg.   Application for Recognition of Exemption Under Section 501(d) or for Determination Under Section 120 (form and instructions);

(2) Form 8718   User Fee for Exempt Organization Determination Letter Request; and

(3) SS-4   Application for Employer Identification Number.

The following are additional free IRS publications that may be of assistance in applying for exempt status:

Publication Number	Title
557	Tax-Exempt Status for Your Organization
598	Tax on Unrelated Business Income of Exempt Organization
892	Exempt Organization Appeal Procedures
990	Return of Organization Exempt from Income Tax
Circular E Publication 15	Employer's Tax Guide
2848	Power of Attorney and Declaration of Representative

2848-D Tax Information Authorization and Declaration of Representative

IV. CITIZEN'S ARREST AND CIVIL LIABILITY

Under the old common law we inherited from England, each citizen has at least some duty to arrest criminals and bring them to justice. Today, most law enforcement has been placed in the hands of professional police, but citizen's arrest retains an important place in the law of every state.

The U.S. Constitution limits law enforcement by the government. To arrest a criminal, the police need to obtain an arrest warrant in advance, approved by a judge. In certain circumstances, policemen may arrest a criminal without a warrant—generally, when the policeman has "probable cause" to believe (a good-faith belief) that a crime has been committed by the person he is about to arrest and that the suspect may flee before a warrant can be obtained. A policeman may also make an arrest without a warrant when a crime is being committed in the policeman's presence. This is the broadest arrest power available to anyone. If a policeman makes a mistake—arresting an innocent person—his good-faith belief that the person was a criminal will protect the policeman from criminal or civil liability for the arrest. That is, the policeman cannot be liable in a civil lawsuit for "false imprisonment" or "deprivation of constitutional rights" (two kinds of tort or personal injury claims), if the policeman made an honest mistake.

Any citizen's arrest is considered an arrest without a warrant. Private citizens, however, are *not* subject to the restraints of the U.S. Constitution, because the limitations of the Bill of Rights apply only to the federal government, the states and those people who are acting under color of government authority. Thus private citizens who claim no official status cannot be liable in a civil action for depriving someone of his *constitutional* rights. But a private citizen may be liable in a civil lawsuit under state law for false arrest or false imprisonment. In this respect, the law is tougher on private citizens than it is on policemen. In most states, there is no "probable cause" or "good faith" allowance for mistakes made in a citizen's arrest. In lawyer's language, a private citizen making an arrest "acts at his own peril." These rules vary greatly, however, from state to state.

In the individual states, various statutes and judicial decisions have created different patterns of modern citizen's arrest law. In many states, the ancient common-law rules handed down from the middle ages apply.[8] In those states, a citizen may arrest a criminal for *any* felony (roughly, a serious crime, punishable by more than a year in jail) and for a misdemeanor committed in the presence of the arresting citizen. Generally, a citizen's arrest may not be made for the violation of a mere municipal ordinance, minor traffic offense or the like.

[8]The term "common law" usually refers to a body of court-made decisional law starting with decisions of the courts of England in the twelfth century. The term is usually used to distinguish court-made decisional law from law arising from statutes enacted by legislatures, although American common law has also included some early English statutory law that has affected court rulings. Historically, most of the law that governed England up until the American Revolution was made by the courts and not by Parliament. In this regard England and her American colonies were unique among western countries; elsewhere, law was made by central governments and incorporated into elaborate statutory codes, like the French *Napoleonic Code* of the early nineteenth century.

Consequently, when I talk about the common-law power of citizen's arrest in this country, I am talking about traditional law that was incorporated into American jurisprudence directly from England during the colonial period and has survived unmodified even in states created long after the American Revolution. For example, West Virginia, which became a separate state in 1863, has a provision in its state constitution that "the common law shall remain in force and effect" until modified by the legislature. Most states, including West Virginia, have interpreted such constitutional provisions as allowing the courts of the state to modify ancient decisional law with modern decisional law to update obsolete rules, but until such time as that occurs, or the legislature enacts a statute controlling a particular subject, the ancient law is good law.

When a person makes a citizen's arrest he or she must be able to take the offender into physical custody. That is why citizen patrols usually have more than one person. In most states a citizen making an arrest can use as much nondeadly force as is necessary to subdue the offender, but the offender can flee or otherwise refuse to be arrested with impunity. When making a citizen's arrest it is important for the arresting person to identify himself or herself and clearly state: "I arrest you in the name of the law for the offense of————." The most common offense for which citizen's arrests are made is shoplifting, but such arrests can also be made for mugging, purse snatching, child molestation, drug dealing, drunken driving and assault. Unless, however, those who would make the arrest have a preponderance of force on their side, so that the offender is unlikely to resist, it is better to attempt only to identify the offender, gather evidence and turn the matter over to the armed police.

Eighteen American jurisdictions follow the common-law rules of citizen's arrest, roughly as outlined earlier, unaltered by statute (although most of these states have statutes expanding a shopkeeper's arrest powers over suspected shoplifters). These states are Connecticut, Delaware, Florida, Kansas, Maine, Maryland, Massachusetts, Missouri, New Hampshire, New Jersey, New Mexico, Pennsylvania, Rhode Island, Virginia, Washington, West Virginia and Wisconsin. The District of Columbia also falls into this category.

States with statutes on citizen's arrest generally treat felonies and misdemeanors differently, and make some provision for mistakes made by the citizen. In one group of states, a citizen's arrest may be made for any misdemeanor committed in the view or presence of the arresting citizen, or for any felony; and the citizen need have only a reasonable belief that the person arrested has committed the offense. These states are Alabama, Alaska, Arizona, California, Idaho, Iowa, Minnesota, Mississippi, Montana, Nevada, North Dakota, Oklahoma, South Dakota, Tennessee and Utah. New York has a similar rule, but mistakes of identity are not forgiven, even if reasonable. In some of these states, a misdemeanor must amount to a breach of the peace, which would probably be the case in the sort of crimes citizen patrols would be interested in (such as open drug-dealing, street-fighting and the like).

In Oregon, a citizen's arrest may be made for any crime, felony or misdemeanor committed in the presence of the arresting citizen, with reasonable mistakes forgiven. In Colorado, Hawaii and Texas, the rule is similar, but mistakes are not forgiven, even if they are reasonable. (In Texas, the crime must amount to a breach of the peace.) In Georgia, a citizen may arrest only a fleeing criminal (misdemeanant or felon), with reasonable mistakes forgiven.

In Illinois, arrest may be made for any misdemeanor or felony, if the citizen reasonably believes that the crime is in the process of being committed. In North Carolina, arrest may be made for any crime causing a breach of the peace, with reasonable mistakes forgiven, but only if the citizen is assisting a policeman.[9] The Michigan rule is similar, but the crime must be a felony, and even reasonable mistakes are not forgiven.

The other states allow citizen's arrest only for felonies, not misdemeanors. In Arkansas, Kentucky, Nebraska, Ohio and Wyoming, arrests are limited to felonies, with reasonable mistakes

[9]Many readers will remember the episode of the Andy Griffith Show in which sheriff's deputy Barney Fife arrested citizen Gomer Pyle for making an illegal U-turn in the peaceful streets of Mayberry, N.C. Moments later, Deputy Fife wheeled his squad car around in the same disfavored traffic pattern. Gomer Pyle, on the scene, shouted "Citizen's ah-ray-yest! Citizen's ah-ray-yest!" and dragged Barney off to the county jail. There, under Sheriff Taylor's direction, Deputy Fife locked himself up in Mayberry's lone jail cell. Everyone learned a valuable lesson: The law applies to lawman and citizen alike. Gomer's arrest of Barney, however, was not lawful. Under the law of North Carolina, Barney's U-turn was merely a violation of a minor local traffic ordinance, not a misdemeanor or felony for which citizen's arrest would be appropriate. Thus, Barney could have filed a civil lawsuit against Gomer for false imprisonment, and Gomer would have been liable for money damages.

forgiven. In Louisiana and South Carolina, mistakes are not forgiven, and the crime must in fact have been committed.

Appendix A includes a chart prepared by Professor M. Cherif Bassiouni for his 1977 book *Citizen's Arrest* [10] outlining the major statutory modifications of the citizen's arrest power made in the states. Appendix A also includes two model statutes, which, if passed by state legislatures, would make citizen's arrest laws uniform and place private citizens on a par with policemen in their power to make arrests. The first statute, drafted by Professor Bassiouni, allows private citizens to arrest on reasonable belief for any crime, misdemeanor or felony, whether or not committed in the arrestor's presence. Reasonable force could be used, but the arrestor would be bound by the same constitutional limits that apply to policemen. These constitutional limits include such stipulations as: (1) in the absence of the offender's use of deadly force (a gun or other weapon), a policeman may not use deadly force to apprehend the offender; (2) a policeman may not arrest a person for a crime not committed in the policeman's presence without a warrant unless there are "exigent circumstances" present that indicate that the if the arrest is not made on the spot the offender will evade capture; (3) the premises, automobile or luggage of an offender cannot be searched without a warrant; (4) the offender must be advised of his right to remain silent and his right to counsel at the time of arrest; and, (5) the offender cannot be interrogated until he has had a chance to meet with his lawyer.

The second statute, drafted for this book, applies to civil suits (such as those for physical injury and false imprisonment) that someone wrongly arrested might bring against the private citizen who arrested him. This second statute incorporates the same good-faith defenses that policemen enjoy in such lawsuits. These two statutes will also make an incorporated citizen crime-control

---

[10]Charles C. Thomas (publisher), Springfield, Ill.

group much more insurable because the liability exposure of citizens would then be roughly the same as that of regular police—a risk about which insurance companies have voluminous actuarial data.

v. Standard Operating Procedures

Citizen crime-prevention groups need to have sensible work rules. This requires leadership and training. The Guardian Angels have specific guidelines for membership in the group and for members' conduct on the job. These rules are summarized here to illustrate one successful approach to citizen policing. The Guardian Angels' rules work well for them, and they work in some of the nation's most dangerous neighborhoods.

To become a Guardian Angel, the prospective member must be at least sixteen years old. He or she must not have any serious criminal record. What is a "serious" criminal record? That must depend on the neighborhood. Crack addiction or car theft would probably disqualify a candidate; simple possession of a small amount of marijuana, or minor vandalism, probably would not be too serious for the Guardian Angels. Given the everyday reality of pervasive crime in some of the Angels' neighborhoods, the Angels cannot be *too* choosy. The Angels' main concern is that the group's reputation not be sullied by involvement with real criminals. The Angels are all volunteers; members must commit themselves to about eight hours of work per week. Members are trained in martial arts, but may not carry any sort of weapon. Each member is searched before he or she goes on patrol; if an Angel is found carrying a weapon or drugs, he or she is permanently expelled from the group.

Guardian Angels are also trained in the laws of citizen's arrest and reasonable force. They do make citizen's arrests for crimes committed in their presence (purse-snatchings, drug-dealing and the like) if they can do so without danger to themselves or others. Each Angel may patrol only in his or her own neighborhood. This prevents the group from being considered a roving band of toughs; it also cements the patrols' relationship with each neighborhood. Citizens naturally think of the group as more legitimate the closer the neighborhood ties between the patrollers and the citizens in the areas patrolled. Similarly, the Angels are trained not to *invite* confrontation. When the group works best, their presence alone is an effective crime deterrent. As a result of the Angels' rigorous training and discipline, people everywhere feel more secure, and indeed *are* more secure, when an Angel in his or her familiar red cap is standing nearby.

The Guardian Angels' way of going about things provides a valuable lesson for other groups in other neighborhoods. Different neighborhoods, however, may have different needs. In a sprawling suburb, for example, car patrols may be more effective than walking patrols. In an area of elderly residents, a crime-prevention group may choose to forego citizen's arrests entirely and focus on watching the streets and neighboring houses from behind the windows of their own houses. In some cases, it may be more effective to join a block-watch program affiliated with the local police department. Such programs have been successful in many cities, most notably Seattle. Block-watch programs do not attempt to do more than serve as extra eyes and ears for the uniformed police.

Another wise tactic employed by the Guardian Angels is to offer some community service other than crime-fighting. The Guardian Angels in Minneapolis, for example, host an annual Thanksgiving feast for the homeless. This is excellent public relations, demonstrating the Guardian Angels' good intentions to everyone in the city. The meal also makes the homeless understand that the Guardian Angels are on their side, too. Although homeless people are often considered a threat by more prosperous people, most of the homeless are not criminals. In fact, they are disproportionately the victims of some of the most brutal street crimes imaginable. The Thanksgiving meal lets the homeless of Minneapolis know that they, too, have a right to be free of crime, and that the Guardian Angels are there to help *them* just as much as to help their more prosperous neighbors. Gestures of good will are bound to work to the benefit of the crime-prevention groups, extending them increased visibility, legitimacy and support.

VI. ARTICLES OF INCORPORATION

Corporations are artificial beings created for specific and limited purposes. Each state has the right to determine the requirements and procedures for a corporation to come into existence, and these requirements and procedures are specified by statute. Similarly the rights, powers and privileges of corporations are conferred by states and are set forth in the laws of each state.

Most states require that the persons setting up a corporation provide certain information to the state about the proposed corporation. This information is generally contained in the articles of incorporation or charter, which must be filed with the appropriate state agency, usually the Secretary of State. Most statutes governing the creation of nonprofit corporations designate the matters to be included in the articles, and the state usually provides a simple form for the articles. My sample articles of incorporation in Appendix B are based on the form provided by the office of the West Virginia Secretary of State. Forms can be obtained from the appropriate state agency.

After the articles of incorporation are filed and the required fees are paid, the state agency reviews the articles to make sure that the corporation described in the articles meets that state's requirements for a nonprofit corporation. The state agency will then issue a certificate of incorporation or a similar notice of acceptance of the charter and record it. It is important to remember that generally the corporation comes into existence only when the state agency issues a certificate of incorporation or notice of acceptance.

In the model articles of incorporation found in Appendix B, I have included the organizational requirements for the recognition of an exemption under section 501(c)(3) of the *Internal Revenue Code* [1986]. I have also noted the sections to be individualized.

VII. CORPORATE BYLAWS

Generally, the bylaws of a nonprofit corporation contain provisions that determine the regulation and management of the affairs of the corporation. The bylaws must be consistent with applicable state corporation law and with the corporation's articles of incorporation. Most states have statutory provisions applicable to nonprofit corporations, and nonprofit corporations must comply with these statutes. For example, Texas requires membership corporations to enact two sets of regulations, a constitution and bylaws. The initial bylaws are generally adopted by the directors. The following articles are often included in bylaws of nonprofit corporations:

1. Name and location of corporation.
2. Membership.
3. Meetings of members and election of officers.
4. Board of Directors.
5. Designation of officers and their duties.
6. Committees.

7. Dues.
8. Resignation and expulsion.
9. Dissolution.
10. Amendments.

A model corporate bylaw form can be found in Appendix B.

STATUTORY ARREST AUTHORITY OF THE PRIVATE CITIZEN

State	Crime	Misdemeanor amounting to a breach of the peace	Breach of the peace	Public offense	Offense	Offense not covered by an ordinance	Indictable offense	Presence	Immediate Knowledge	View	Upon reasonable grounds that a crime is being committed	Felony	Larceny	Petit larceny	Crime involving physical injury to another	Crime	Crime involving theft or destruction of property	Committed in presence	Information that a felony has been committed	View	Reasonable grounds to believe a felony is being committed	That felony has been committed in fact	The felon is escaping or attempting escape	Summoned by peace officer to assist in arrest	The felon is in the act of committing	Reasonable grounds to believe the person arrested committed the crime	Probable cause
	MINOR OFFENSE											MAJOR OFFENSE												CERTAINTY OF CORRECT ARREST			
	Type of Minor Offense							Type of Knowledge Required				Type of Major Offense						Type of Knowledge Required									
Alabama				X				X				X										X				X	
Alaska	X							X				X										X				X	
Arizona		X						X				X										X				X	
Arkansas												X									X					X	
California				X				X				X										X				X	
Colorado	X							X								X		X									
Georgia				X				X	X			X						X						X		X	
Hawaii	X							X								X		X							X		
Idaho				X				X				X										X				X	
Illinois							X				X	X									X						
Iowa				X				X				X										X				X	
Kentucky												X										X				X	
Louisiana												X										X					
Michigan												X						X				X		X			
Minnesota			X					X				X										X				X	
Mississippi		X					X	X				X										X				X	
Montana					X			X				X										X				X	
Nebraska												X	X									X				X	
Nevada				X				X				X										X				X	
New York					X			X				X										X					
N. Carolina*		X										X			X		X								X		X
N. Dakota				X				X				X										X				X	
Ohio												X								X		X				X	
Oklahoma				X				X				X										X				X	
Oregon	X							X								X		X									X
S. Carolina												X	X					X	X			X					
S. Dakota				X				X				X										X				X	
Tennessee				X				X				X										X				X	
Texas		X						X	X			X						X	X								
Utah				X				X				X										X				X	
Wyoming												X		X								X				X	

*The statute eliminates the use of the word *arrest* and replaces it with *detention*.

From M. Cherif Bassiouni, *Citizen's Arrest*, 1977.
Courtesy of Charles C. Thomas, Publisher, Springfield, Illinois.

Appendix A:

MODEL STATUTES

I. STATUTORY ARREST AUTHORITY OF THE PRIVATE CITIZEN

ii. Model Citizen's Arrest Statute[11]

(1) Any person other than an authorized public officer as defined by [the laws of the state] may arrest another for any offense [crime or violation] as defined by [the law of the state or any political subdivision thereof] other than a quasicriminal violation and municipal ordinance subject to the requirements and limitations set forth in this statute

(2) Any such arrest can be made on reasonable grounds to believe that the offense has been committed or is being committed and

[11]Copyright 1977, Charles C. Thomas, Publisher. Reprinted with the kind permission of the publisher and author.

the arrestor has reasonable grounds to believe the arrestee has committed, is committing or is about to commit said offense.

(3) The arrestor must give the arrestee notice of his or her intention to perform the arrest and state the reasons therefore.

(4) The arrestor may in effectuating the arrest use any reasonable amount of force necessary and warranted under the circumstances other than deadly force and force causing great bodily harm, but without prejudice to the right of "self-defense."

(5) The arrestee shall not resist the arrest unless he knows it to be unlawful. This shall not, however, prejudice the arrestee's right to "self-defense" in preventing any unauthorized harm from occurring to him or her.

(6) An arrestor must, upon performing the arrest, notify a peace officer and deliver the arrestee to the custody of public authorities without delay.

(7) The arrestor, regardless of his or her identity or authority, shall be subject to the same constitutional and statutory limitations imposed on public agents with regard to unreasonable searches and seizure and the privilege against self-incrimination.

(8) A reasonable mistake of fact or law shall be a defense to the arrestor.

(9) The following categories of public officials are immune from citizen's arrest:

  a. law enforcement agents (local, state, federal),
  b. members of the judiciary (local, state, federal),
  c. members of the legislature (local, state, federal),
  d. (others to be specified by each state).

(10) This statute abrogates any prior legislation and supersedes any inconsistent legislation and public policy.

III. MODEL CITIZEN CRIME PATROL STATUTE

Section One

The Secretary of State (or other appropriate official) of this State shall maintain a record of certified citizen crime patrol groups active in this state. To be so certified, such a group must offer proof that:

(a) It is organized as an unincorporated association or nonprofit corporation under the laws of this State.

(b) Its primary purpose is the prevention or detection of crime, or the apprehension of persons committing crimes in the presence of a member of the group;

(c) Its members, in their capacity as such, do not carry firearms or other deadly offensive weapons;

(d) Its members restrict their actions to the community or neighborhood in which all the members live or work; and

(e) Its membership criteria are not political, racial, religious or ethnic in nature and both sexes are admitted to membership on equal terms.

Section Two

In civil tort actions:

(a) A certified citizen crime-patrol group and its members shall enjoy any and all statutory or common-law immunities or defenses available to municipal policemen, state troopers or sheriffs and their deputies under the laws of this State, in addition to such immunities or defenses they may enjoy as private persons;

(b) Notwithstanding that a group has not been certified under Section One of this Act, subsection 2(a) of this act shall apply to such group and its members if in any suit or proceeding the trial judge finds by a preponderance of the evidence that the group meets the criteria set forth in Section One of this Act.

Appendix B:

FORMS FOR NONPROFIT CORPORATIONS

I. MODEL ARTICLES OF INCORPORATION

ARTICLES OF INCORPORATION

of

_____

The undersigned, acting as incorporator(s) of a corporation under the State of _____ adopt(s) the following Articles of Incorporation for such corporation:[12]

   1. The undersigned agree to become a nonprofit corporation by the name of

_____ .[13]

---

[12]Reference should be made to the appropriate state law. Most states have either suggested or statutory official forms of articles of incorporation. These forms can be generally obtained from the office of the Secretary of State or other state agency. Our suggested form is based on the form supplied by the office of the Secretary of State for West Virginia.

[13]Some states require that the corporation's name contain a word indicating its status

2. A. The address at the physical location of the principal office of the corporation will be _____
street, in the city, town or village of _____ , county of
_____ ,State of _____ , Zip Code _____ .
The mailing address of the above location, if different, will be _____ .
B. The address at the physical location of the principal place of business in _____
of the corporation, if different than the above address, will be _____
street, in the city, town or village of _____ , _____
County, _____ , Zip Code _____ . The mailing
address of the above location, if different, will be _____ .[14]

3. This corporation is organized as a nonprofit public-benefit corporation with the limitations of section 501(c)(3) of the *Internal Revenue Code* [1986] or corresponding section of any future tax code.[15]

4. The period of duration of the corporation, which may be perpetual, is

_____ .

5. The purpose for which this corporation is formed is:

To promote, encourage and foster the common good and general welfare of the people of the United States through a program of prevention and suppression of crime; thereby, lessening the burdens of government and lessening neighborhood tensions within the limits of section 501(c)(3) of the *Internal Revenue Code* [1986], or the corresponding section of any future federal tax code.[16]

as a corporation. For example: "Inc." "corporation," "company," "foundation," "incorporated," "limited" or an abbreviation of one of these words.

The availability of the selected name should be checked with the appropriate state agency; two corporations cannot use the same name.

[14]Some states require that a copy of the articles of incorporation be filed not only with the centralized state agency, but also in the county where the principal place of business is located.

[15]Organizations that are exempt from federal income tax under section 501(a) of the *Internal Revenue Code* [1986] (the Code) include the organizations described in section 501(c) of the Code. Donations made exclusively for public purposes to an organization described in section 501(c)(3) of the Code are deductible on the donor's federal income tax.

[16]To qualify for recognition of the exemption under the *Internal Revenue Code*, the corporation's articles of incorporation must (1) limit the organization's purposes to those described in section 501(c)(3) of the *Code*; (2) limit the corporation's political activities; (3) insure that no part of the corporation's earnings inure to the benefit of members as individuals; and (4) insure that the corporation is not organized or operated for the benefit of private interests.

Additional purposes can be added, if desired. However, any additional purposes should be drafted to conform to the requirements of section 501(c) of the *Internal Revenue Code*.

6. The provisions for the regulation of the internal affairs of the corporation, which the incorporators elect to set forth in the articles of incorporation, are as follows:

No part of the net earnings of the corporation shall inure to the benefit of, or be distributable to its members, trustees, officers or other private persons, except that the corporation shall be authorized and empowered to pay reasonable compensation for services rendered to make payments and distributions in furtherance of the purposes set forth in Article Five hereof. No substantial part of the activities of the corporation shall be the carrying on of propaganda, or otherwise attempting to influence legislation, and the corporation shall not participate in, or intervene in (including the publishing or distribution of statements) any political campaign on behalf of or in opposition to any candidate for public office. Notwithstanding any other provision of these articles, the corporation shall not carry on any other activities not permitted to be carried on (a) by a corporation exempt from federal income tax under section 501(c)(3) of the *Internal Revenue Code*, or corresponding section of any future federal tax code, or (b) by a corporation, contributions to which are deductible under section 170(c)(2) of the *Internal Revenue Code*, or corresponding section of any future federal tax code.

Upon the dissolution of the corporation, assets shall be distributed for one or more exempt purposes within the meaning of section 501(c)(3) of the *Internal Revenue Code*, or corresponding section of any future federal tax code, or shall be distributed to the federal government, or to a state or local government, for a public purpose. Any such assets not so disposed of shall be disposed of by the Circuit Court of the county in which the principal office of the corporation is then located, exclusively for such purposes or to such organization or organizations, as said Court shall determine, which are organized and operated exclusively for such purposes.[17]

7. The full name(s) and address(es) of the incorporator(s), including street and street numbers, if any, and the city, town or village, including the zip code, and the number of shares subscribed for by each is (are) as follows:

NAME   ADDRESS

_____

_____ [18]

---

[17]To establish an exemption under section 501(c)(3) of the Code, a corporation must permanently dedicate its assets to exempt purposes. In certain situations an express provision for distribution of assets upon dissolution is not required in the articles of incorporation.

In West Virginia, Circuit Courts are the trial courts of general jurisdiction. Other states use different names for such courts, for example, Court of Common Pleas. The appropriate court title should be inserted.

[18]An incorporator is the person who submits the articles of incorporation for filing. Acting as an incorporator does not mean that person will run the corporation.

8. The number of directors constituting the initial board of directors of the corporation is _____ and the names and addresses of the persons who are to serve as directors until the first annual meeting of members, or until their successors are elected and shall qualify, are as follows:

NAME   ADDRESS

_____

_____

_____

_____

_____ .[19]

_____

9. The name and address of the appointed person to whom notice or process may be sent is _____

_____ .

ACKNOWLEDGMENT

I (We), the undersigned, for the purpose of forming a corporation under the laws of the State of _____ , do make and file these "Articles of Incorporation."

In witness whereof, I (we) have accordingly hereunto set my (our) respective hand(s) this _____ day of _____ , 19 _____ .

(All incorporators must sign below. Names and signatures must appear the same throughout the Articles of Incorporation.)[20]

_____

_____   _____

STATE OF _____
COUNTY OF _____

I, _____ , a Notary Public, in and for the county and state aforesaid, hereby certify that (names of all incorporators as shown in item 7 must be inserted in this space by official taking acknowledgement) whose name(s) is (are) signed to the foregoing Articles of Incorporation, this day personally appeared before me in my said county and acknowledged his (her) (their) signature(s).

[19]Some states require a minimum number of people be in the corporation; for example, the president and the secretary must not be the same person.

[20]A number of states require that the signatures of the incorporators and the notary public be original in all copies submitted to the state agency.

My commission expires _____

_____
(Notary Public)

PREPARED BY _____ ,[21]

_____
(Name)

_____
(Address)

II. MODEL CORPORATE BYLAWS

Bylaws of _____

ARTICLE I. OFFICES

The principal office of the corporation in the State of _____ shall be located in the City of _____ , County of _____ . The corporation may have such other offices, either within or without the State of _____ , as the board of directors may determine or as the affairs of the corporation may require from time to time.

The corporation shall have and continuously maintain in the State of _____ a registered office, and a registered agent whose office is identical with such registered office, as required by the _____ Nonprofit Corporation Act. The registered office may be, but need not be, identical with the principal office in the State of _____ , and the address of the registered office may be changed from time to time by the board of directors.

ARTICLE II. MEMBERS

Section 1. Class of Members. The corporation shall have one class of members. Membership reflects a contribution to or a commitment to participate in the support the public-benefit goals of the corporation.

Section 2. Election of Members. A member, with his or her consent, shall be elected

[21]The preparer of the articles of incorporation should be identified.

207

by the board of directors.[22] An affirmative vote of two-thirds of the directors shall be required for election.

Section 3. Voting Rights. Each member shall be entitled to one vote on each matter submitted to a vote of the members.

Section 4. Termination of Membership. The board of directors, by affirmative vote of two-thirds of all of the members of the board, may suspend or expel a member for cause after an appropriate notice and hearing, and may, by a majority vote of those present at any regularly constituted meeting, terminate the membership of any member who becomes ineligible for membership, or suspend or expel any member who shall be in default in the payment of dues for the period fixed in Article XI of these bylaws.

Section 5. Resignation. Any member may resign by filing a written resignation with the secretary, but such resignation shall not relieve the member so resigning of the obligation to pay any dues, assessments or other charges theretofore accrued and unpaid.

Section 6. Reinstatement. Upon written request signed by a former member and filed with the secretary, the board of directors may, by the affirmative vote of two-thirds of the members of the board, reinstate such former member to membership upon such terms as the board of directors may deem appropriate.[23]

Section 7. Transfer of Membership. Membership in this corporation is not transferable or assignable.[24]

Section 8. Liability of Members. Members of this corporation are not, as such, personally liable for the acts, debts, liabilities or obligations of this corporation.

ARTICLE III. MEETINGS OF MEMBERS

Section 1. Annual Meeting. An annual meeting of the members shall be held on the _____ in the month of _____ in each year, beginning with the year 19 _____ , at the hour of _____ o'clock, ___ .M., for the purpose of electing directors and for the transaction of such other business as may come before the meeting. If the day fixed for the annual meeting shall be a legal holiday in the State of _____ , such meeting shall be held on the next succeeding business day. If the election of directors shall not be held on the day designated herein for any annual meeting of the members, then it shall be held as soon thereafter as conveniently may be.

---

[22]The board of directors may require that prospective participating members meet specific requirements, such as minimum age and lack of a criminal record. *See infra* p. 00 discussion of Guardian Angel's membership guidelines.

[23]If desired, the bylaws can specify a different affirmative vote by the board of directors on membership matters, for example a majority.

[24]If the transfer of membership is desired the following provision may be used:

Any membership in this corporation may be transferred and assigned by a member whose dues are paid in full, to any person who has met the membership requirements, is approved by the board of directors and elected to membership.

Section 2. Special Meetings. Special meetings of the members may be called by the president, the board of directors, or not less than one-tenth of the members.

Section 3. Place of Meeting. The board of directors may designate any place, either within or without the State of _____ , as the place of meeting for any annual meeting or for any special meeting called by the board of directors. If no designation is made or if a special meeting be otherwise called, the place of meeting shall be the registered office of the corporation in the State of _____ ; but if all of the members shall meet at any time and place, either within or without the State of _____ , and consent to the holding of a meeting, such meeting shall be valid without call or notice, and at such meeting any corporate action may be taken.

Section 4. Notice of meetings. Written or printed notice stating the place, day and hour of any meeting of members shall be delivered, either personally or by mail, to each member listed with the secretary on the business day preceding the day on which notice is given, not less than 10 nor more than 50 days before the date of such meeting, by or at the direction of the president, or the secretary, or the officers or persons calling the meeting. In case of a special meeting or when required by statute or by these bylaws, the purpose or purposes for which the meeting is called shall be stated in the notice. If mailed, the notice of the meeting shall be deemed to be delivered when deposited in the United States mail addressed to the member at his address as it appears on the records of the corporation, with proper postage.[25]

Section 5. Informal Action by Members. Any action required by law to be taken at a meeting of the members, or any action which may be taken at a meeting of members, may be taken without a meeting if a consent in writing, setting forth the action so taken, shall be signed by all of the members entitled to vote with respect to the subject matter thereof.

Section 6. Quorum. The members holding one-tenth of the votes which may be present at any meeting shall constitute a quorum at such meeting. If a quorum is not present at any meeting of members, a majority of the members present may adjourn the meeting from time to time without further notice.[26]

Section 7. Proxies. At any meeting of members, a member entitled to vote may vote by proxy executed in writing by the member or by his duly authorized attorney in fact. No proxy shall be valid after 11 months from the date of its execution, unless otherwise provided in the proxy.

Section 8. Voting by Mail. The election of directors or officers by members may be conducted by mail in such manner as the board of directors shall determine.

[25]If desired, a different notice can be required, assuming the requirements of state law are met.

[26]If a corporation has membership attendance problems, the bylaw may define a quorum as those members attending or voting upon a matter.

ARTICLE IV. BOARD OF DIRECTORS

Section 1. General Powers. The affairs of the corporation shall be managed by its board of directors. Directors need not be residents of the State of _____ or members of the corporation.

Section 2. Number, Tenure and Qualifications. The number of directors shall be at least three.[27] Each director shall hold office until the next annual meeting of members and until his successor shall have been elected and qualified.

Section 3. Regular Meetings. A regular annual meeting of the board of directors shall be held without other notice than this bylaw, immediately after, and at the same place as, the annual meeting of members. The board of directors may provide by resolution the time and place, either within or without the State of _____ , for the holding of additional regular meetings of the board without notice other than the resoluton.

Section 4. Special Meetings. Special meetings of the board of directors may be called by or at the request of the president or any two directors. The person or persons authorized to call special meetings of the board may fix any place, either within or without the State of _____, as the place for holding any special meeting or the board called by them.

Section 5. Notice. Notice of any special meeting of the board of directors shall be given at least two days before such meeting by written notice delivered personally or sent by mail or telegram to each director at the address as shown by the records of the corporation. If mailed, such notice shall be deemed to be delivered when deposited in the United States mail in a sealed envelope so addressed, with proper postage. Any director may waive notice of any meeting. The attendance of a director at any meeting shall constitute a waiver of notice of such meeting, except where a director attends a meeting for the express purpose of objecting to the transaction of any business because the meeting is not lawfully called or convened. Neither the business to be transacted at, nor the purpose of, any regular or special meeting of the board need be specified in the notice or waiver of notice of such meeting, unless specifically required by law.

Section 6. Quorum. A majority of the board of directors shall constitute a quorum for the transaction of business at any meeting of the board; but if less than a majority of the directors is present at said meeting, a majority of the directors present may adjourn the meeting from time to time without further notice.[28]

---

[27]The number of directors may be increased or decreased and the number can be changed by amending the bylaws as provided in Article XV of these bylaws. The directors named in the articles of incorporation generally hold office until the first annual meeting of the members.

[28]Although the bylaws may define any number attending as a quorum, realistically, the quorum should not consist of less than one-third of the board of directors.

Section 7. Manner of Acting. The act of a majority of the directors present at a meeting at which a quorum is present shall be the act of the board of directors, unless the act of a greater number is required by law.

Section 8. Vacancies. Any vacancy occurring in the board of directors and any directorship to be filled by reason of an increase in the number of directors, shall be filled by the board of directors. A director elected to fill a vacancy shall be elected for the unexpired term of his predecessor in office.

Section 9. Compensation. Directors as such shall not receive any stated salaries for their services, but by resolution of the board of directors a fixed sum and expenses of attendance, if any, may be allowed for attendance at each regular or special meeting of the board; but nothing herein contained shall be construed to preclude any director from serving the corporation in any other capacity and receiving compensation therefor.

Section 10. Informal Action by Directors. Any action required by law to be taken at a meeting of directors, or any action which may be taken at a meeting of directors, may be taken without a meeting if a consent in writing, setting forth the action so taken, shall be signed by all of the directors.

ARTICLE V. OFFICERS

Section 1. Officers. The officers of the corporation shall be a president, one or more vice-presidents (the number thereof to be determined by the board of directors), a secretary, a treasurer and such other officers as may be elected in accordance with the provisions of this article. The board of directors may elect or appoint such other officers, including one or more assistant secretaries and one or more assistant treasurers, as it shall deem desirable, such officers to have the authority and perform the duties prescribed, from time to time, by the board of directors. Any two or more offices may be held by the same person, except the offices of president and secretary.

Section 2. Election and Term of Office. The officers of the corporation shall be elected annually by the board of directors at the regular annual meeting of the board of directors. If the election of officers shall not be held at such meeting, such election shall be held as soon thereafter as is convenient. New offices may be created and filled at any meeting of the board of directors. Each officer shall hold office until his successor shall have been duly elected and shall have qualified.

Section 3. Removal. Any officer elected or appointed by the board of directors may be removed by the board of directors whenever in its judgment the best interests of the corporation would be served thereby, but such removal shall be without prejudice to the contract rights, if any, of the officer so removed.

Section 4. Vacancies. A vacancy in any office because of death, resignation, removal, disqualification or otherwise, may be filled by the board of directors for the unexpired portion of the term.

Section 5. President. The president shall be the principal executive officer of the corporation and shall in general supervise and control all of the business and affairs of the corporation. He shall preside at all meetings of the members of the board of directors. He may sign, with the secretary or any other proper officer of the corporation authorized by the board of directors, any deeds, mortgages, bonds, contracts, or other instruments which the board of directors has authorized to be executed, except in cases where the signing and execution thereof shall be expressly delegated by the board of directors or by statute to some other officer or agent of the corporation; and in general he shall perform all duties incident to the office of president and such other duties as may be prescribed by the board of directors from time to time.

Section 6. Vice-President. In the absence of the president or in event of his inability or refusal to act, the vice-president (or in the event there be more than one vice-president, the vice-presidents in the order of their election) shall perform the duties of the president, and when so acting, shall have all the powers of and be subject to all the restrictions upon the president. Any vice-president shall perform such other duties as from time to time may be assigned to him by the president or by the board of directors.

Section 7. Treasurer. If required by the board of directors, the treasurer shall give a bond for the faithful discharge of his duties in such sum and with such surety or sureties as the board of directors shall determine. He shall have charge and custody of and be responsible for all funds and securities of the corporation; receive and give receipts for moneys due and payable to the corporation from any source whatsoever, and deposit all such moneys in the name of the corporation in such banks, trust companies or other depositaries as shall be selected in accordance with the provisions of Article VII of these bylaws; and in general perform all the duties incident to the office of treasurer and such other duties as from time to time may be assigned to him by the president or by the board of directors.

Section 8. Secretary. The secretary shall keep the minutes of the meetings of the members and of the board of directors in one or more books provided for that purpose; see that all notices are duly given in accordance with the provisions of these bylaws or as required by law; be custodian of the corporate records and of the seal of the corporation and see that the seal of the corporation is affixed to all documents, the execution of which on behalf of the corporation under its seal is duly authorized in accordance with the provisions of these bylaws; keep a register of the post office address of each member which shall be furnished to the secretary by such member; and in general perform all duties incident to the office of secretary and such other duties as from time to time may be assigned to him by the president or by the board of directors.

Section 9. Assistant Treasurers and Assistant Secretaries. If required by the board of directors, the assistant treasurers shall give bonds for the faithful discharge of their duties in such sums and with such sureties as the board of directors shall determine. The assistant treasurers and assistant secretaries, in general, shall perform such duties as shall be assigned to them by the treasurer or the secretary or by the president or the board of directors.

ARTICLE VI. COMMITTEES

Section 1. Committees of Directors. The board of directors, by resolution adopted by a majority of the directors in office, may designate and appoint one or more committees, each of which shall consist of two or more directors, which committees, to the extent provided in said resolution, shall have and exercise the authority of the board of directors in the management of the corporation; provided, however, that no such committee shall have the authority of the board of directors in reference to amending, altering or repealing the bylaws; electing, appointing or removing any member of any such committee or any director or officer of the corporation; amending the articles of incorporation; adopting a plan of merger or adopting a plan of consolidation with another corporation; authorizing the sale, lease, exchange or mortgage of all or substantially all of the property and assets of the corporation; authorizing the voluntary dissolution of the corporation or revoking proceedings therefor; adopting a plan for the distribution of the assets of the corporation; or amending, altering or repealing any resolution of the board of directors which by its terms provides that it shall not be amended, altered or repealed by such committee. The designation and appointment of any such committee and the delegation thereto of authority shall not operate to relieve the board of directors, or any individual director, of any responsibility imposed upon it or the individual by law.

Section 2. Other Committees. Other committees not having and exercising the authority of the board of directors in the management of the corporation may be designated by a resolution adopted by a majority of the directors present at a which a quorum is present. Except as otherwise provided in such resolution, members of each such committee shall be members of the corporation, and the president of the corporation shall appoint the members thereof. Any member thereof may be removed by the person or persons authorized to appoint such member whenever in their judgment the best interests of the corporation shall be served by such removal.

Section 3. Term of office. Each member of a committee shall continue as such until the next annual meeting of the members of the corporation and until his successor is appointed, unless the committee shall be sooner terminated, or unless such member be removed from such committee, or unless such member shall cease to qualify as a member thereof.

Section 4. Chairman. One member of each committee shall be appointed chairman by the person or persons authorized to appoint the members thereof.

Section 5. Vacancies. Vacancies in the membership of any committee may be filled by appointments made in the same manner as provided in the case of the original appointments.

Section 6. Quorum. Unless otherwise provided in the resolution of the board of directors designating a committee, a majority of the whole committee shall constitute a quorum and the act of a majority of the members present at a meeting at which a quorum is present shall be the act of the committee.

Section 7. Rules. Each committee may adopt rules for its own government not inconsistent with these bylaws or with rules adopted by the board of directors.

ARTICLE VII. CONTRACTS, CHECKS, DEPOSITS AND FUNDS

Section 1. Contracts. The board of directors may authorize any officer or officers, agent or agents of the corporation, in addition to the officers so authorized by these bylaws, to enter into any contract or execute and deliver any instrument in the name of and on behalf of the corporation, and such authority may be general or confined to specific instances.

Section 2. Checks, Drafts, etc. All checks, drafts or orders for the payment of money, notes or other evidence in indebtedness issued in the name of the corporation, shall be signed by such officer or officers, agent or agents of the corporation and in such manner as shall from time to time be determined by resolution of the board of directors. In the absence of such determination by the board of directors, such instruments shall be signed by the treasurer or an assistant treasurer and countersigned by the president or a vice-president of the corporation.

Section 3. Deposits. All funds of the corporation shall be deposited from time to time to the credit of the corporation in such banks, trust companies or other depositaries as the board of directors may select.

Section 4. Gifts. The board of directors may accept on behalf of the corporation any contribution, gift, bequest or devise for the general purposes or for any special purpose of the corporation.

ARTICLE VIII. CERTIFICATES OF MEMBERSHIP

Section 1. Certificates of Membership. The board of directors may provide for the issuance of certificates evidencing membership in the corporation, which shall be in such form as may be determined by the board. Such certificates shall be signed by the president or a vice-president and by the secretary or an assistant secretary and shall be sealed with the seal of the corporation. All certificates evidencing membership shall be consecutively numbered. The name and address of each member and the date of issuance of the certificate shall be entered on the records of the corporation. If any certificate shall become lost, mutilated or destroyed, a new certificate may be issued therefor upon such terms and conditions as the board of directors may determine.

Section 2. Issuance of Certificates. When a member has been elected to membership and has paid any initiation fee and dues that may then be required, a certificate of membership shall be issued in his name and delivered to him by the secretary, if the board of directors shall have provided for the issuance of certificates of membership under the provisions of Section 1 of this Article VIII.

ARTICLE IX. BOOKS AND RECORDS

The corporation shall keep correct and complete books and records of account and shall also keep minutes of the proceedings of its members, board of directors and committees having any of the authority of the board of directors, and shall keep at the registered or principal office a record giving the names and addresses of the members entitled to vote. All books and records of the corporation may be inspected by any member, or his agent or attorney for any proper purpose at any reasonable time.

ARTICLE X. FISCAL YEAR

The fiscal year of the corporation shall begin on the first day of January and end on the last day of December in each year.

ARTICLE XI. DUES

Section 1. Annual Dues. The board of directors may determine from time to time the amount of initiation fee, if any, and annual dues payable to the corporation by members.

Section 2. Payment of Dues. Dues shall be payable in advance on the first day of January in each fiscal year. Dues of a new member shall be prorated from the first day of the month in which such new member is elected to membership, for the remainder of the fiscal year of the corporation.

Section 3. Default and Termination of Membership. When any member of any class shall be in default in the payment of dues for a period of _____ months from the beginning of the fiscal year or period for which such dues become payable, his membership may thereupon be terminated by the board of directors in the manner provided in Article III of these bylaws.

ARTICLE XII. SEAL

The board of directors shall provide a corporate seal, which shall be in the form of a circle and shall have inscribed thereon the name of the corporation and the words "Corporate Seal. _____ ."

ARTICLE XIII. WAIVER OF NOTICE

Whenever any notice is required to be given under the provisions of the _____ Nonprofit Corporation Act or under the provisions of the articles of incorporation or the bylaws of the corporation, a waiver thereof in writing signed by the person or persons entitled to such notice, whether before or after the time stated therein, shall be deemed equivalent to the giving of such notice.

ARTICLE XIV. DISSOLUTION

In the event of the dissolution or final liquidation of the corporation, none of the property of the corporation nor any proceeds thereof shall be distributed to or divided among any of the directors, officers or members of the corporation or inure to the benefit of any individual.

After all liabilities and obligations of the corporation have been paid, satisfied and discharged, or adequate provision made therefor, all remaining property and assets of the corporation shall be distributed. Upon the dissolution of the corporation, assets shall be distributed for one or more exempt purposes within the meaning of section 501(c)(3) of the *Internal Revenue Code*, or corresponding section of any future federal tax code, or shall be distributed to the federal government, or to a state or local government, for a public purpose. Any such assets not so disposed of shall be disposed of by the Circuit Court of the county in which the principal office of the corporation is then located, exclusively for such purposes or to such organization or organizations, as said Court shall determine, which are organized and operated exclusively for such purposes.[29]

ARTICLE XV. AMENDMENTS TO BYLAWS

These bylaws may be altered, amended or repealed and new bylaws may be adopted by a majority of the directors present at any regular meeting or at any special meeting, if at least two days' written notice is given of intention to alter, amend or repeal or to adopt new bylaws at such meeting.

[29]If the sample articles of incorporation are used, this section on dissolution can be deleted.

Index